SELF-LEARNING MANAGEMENT SERIES

BUSINESS PLAN ESSENTIALS

YOU ALWAYS WANTED TO KNOW

A practical guide for business students, entrepreneurs, and veteran business owners for creating an effective business plan

DR. ANNAMARIA BLIVEN

Edited by **Mark Koscinski**

Business Plan Essentials You Always Wanted To Know

First Edition

Paperback ISBN 10: 1-63651-121-X
Paperback ISBN 13: 978-1-63651-121-4

Ebook ISBN 10: 1-63651-122-8
Ebook ISBN 13: 978-1-63651-122-1

Hardback ISBN 10: 1-63651-123-6
Hardback ISBN 13: 978-1-63651-123-8

Library of Congress Control Number: 2022938404

This publication is designed to provide accurate and authoritative information in regard to the subject matter covered. The Author has made every effort in the preparation of this book to ensure the accuracy of the information. However, information in this book is sold without warranty either expressed or implied. The Author or the Publisher will not be liable for any damages caused or alleged to be caused either directly or indirectly by this book.

Vibrant Publishers books are available at special quantity discount for sales promotions, or for use in corporate training programs. For more information please write to bulkorders@vibrantpublishers.com

Please email feedback / corrections (technical, grammatical or spelling) to spellerrors@vibrantpublishers.com

To access the complete catalogue of Vibrant Publishers, visit www.vibrantpublishers.com

SELF-LEARNING MANAGEMENT SERIES

TITLE	PAPERBACK* ISBN
ACCOUNTING, FINANCE & ECONOMICS	
COST ACCOUNTING AND MANAGEMENT ESSENTIALS	9781636511030
FINANCIAL ACCOUNTING ESSENTIALS	9781636510972
FINANCIAL MANAGEMENT ESSENTIALS	9781636511009
MACROECONOMICS ESSENTIALS	9781636511818
MICROECONOMICS ESSENTIALS	9781636511153
PERSONAL FINANCE ESSENTIALS	9781636511849
ENTREPRENEURSHIP & STRATEGY	
BUSINESS PLAN ESSENTIALS	9781636511214
BUSINESS STRATEGY ESSENTIALS	9781949395778
ENTREPRENEURSHIP ESSENTIALS	9781636511603
GENERAL MANAGEMENT	
BUSINESS LAW ESSENTIALS	9781636511702
DECISION MAKING ESSENTIALS	9781636510026
LEADERSHIP ESSENTIALS	9781636510316
PRINCIPLES OF MANAGEMENT ESSENTIALS	9781636511542
TIME MANAGEMENT ESSENTIALS	9781636511665

*Also available in Hardback & Ebook formats

SELF-LEARNING MANAGEMENT SERIES

TITLE	PAPERBACK* ISBN
HUMAN RESOURCE MANAGEMENT	
DIVERSITY IN THE WORKPLACE ESSENTIALS	9781636511122
HR ANALYTICS ESSENTIALS	9781636510347
HUMAN RESOURCE MANAGEMENT ESSENTIALS	9781949395839
ORGANIZATIONAL BEHAVIOR ESSENTIALS	9781636510378
ORGANIZATIONAL DEVELOPMENT ESSENTIALS	9781636511481
MARKETING & SALES MANAGEMENT	
DIGITAL MARKETING ESSENTIALS	9781949395747
MARKETING MANAGEMENT ESSENTIALS	9781636511788
SALES MANAGEMENT ESSENTIALS	9781636510743
SERVICES MARKETING ESSENTIALS	9781636511733
OPERATIONS & PROJECT MANAGEMENT	
AGILE ESSENTIALS	9781636510057
OPERATIONS & SUPPLY CHAIN MANAGEMENT ESSENTIALS	9781949395242
PROJECT MANAGEMENT ESSENTIALS	9781636510712
STAKEHOLDER ENGAGEMENT ESSENTIALS	9781636511511

*Also available in Hardback & Ebook formats

About the Author

Dr. AnnaMaria has worked as a business professional for over 30 years gaining experience in business development and management, business improvement, project management, career development and advancement, business strategy, vet-entrepreneurship, team development, teaching and training, and implementation of community projects, and many more lessons learned in starting and sustaining for-profit and not-for-profit businesses.

As a seasoned business owner, her goals are to share lessons and best practices for starting, sustaining, and succeeding in business ventures. To that end, she meets with clients on a regular basis assisting them with achieving their career and business goals. Dr. Bliven started her career as a Certified Travel Consultant while in the Army National Guard and served a total of 26 years with combined service in the Army National Guard, Army, and Army Reserve in the career fields of music, human resources, and education services, and career development. She achieved her Certification as a Global Career Development Facilitator in addition to becoming a Data Analyst and a college instructor. She has an undergraduate degree in Communication from Arizona State University, a Master of Arts degree in Communication from West Virginia University, a Master's in Business Administration from Colorado Technical University-online, and a Doctorate in Business Administration from the University of Wisconsin-Whitewater.

Other contributors

We would like to thank our editor, Mark Koscinski, for his contribution to making this book the best version possible. Mark has over 40 years of experience in accounting and management. He has degrees in economics, accounting, taxation, and personal financial planning. He also maintains an active consulting practice. He is the author of Decision Making Essentials You Always Wanted to Know from the Self-Learning Management series and is also on the Editorial Advisory Board at Vibrant Publishers.

What experts say about this book!

Teaching business planning for thirty years has forced me to be highly selective when considering a textbook, template, or software purporting to be helpful to new business plan writers. Most of these products are not easy and helpful because they offer too much or too little and are often vague as a foggy day on the coast or filled with whitewash. Business Plan Essentials caught my eye and interest quickly because it is precisely the kind of material I want my students and clients to work with for a successful outcome. It is organized in the correct order and every section offers a sweeping view but in language anyone can understand. This book guides the reader to think like the person who will read their plan and provides unique examples of business planning beyond a business startup. The vocabulary and sentence structure are readable and understandable for an average reader. Business Plan Essentials is a clear guide that is easy to read and understand by anyone. It lays out every essential step in writing a compelling business plan for any business situation. This book is a 'keeper' and like a knowledgeable friend, is ready to answer your planning questions in clear and common language. Business Plan Essentials is the easy-to-use business planning book I wanted for my students and clients.

– Stephen O'Mara, Professor of Business Entrepreneurship, Mendocino College

Business Plan Essentials offers a solid synthesis of the approach to business plans. The covered methods are relevant to students of entrepreneurship as well as business owners. The succinct nature of the book allows readers to gain a quick understanding of the concepts, and the use of discussion questions and quizzes at the end of each chapter encourages reflection and a better understanding of the material. Everyone interested in preparing a business plan or starting a business can benefit from this book, which also offers practical examples and solutions to many questions new and budding entrepreneurs have.

– Arkadiusz Mironko, Assistant Professor of Management, Indiana University East

What experts say about this book!

Business Plan Essentials breaks down the core components of creating a forward-looking plan, describing and planning strategies in a way that any reader from students to new entrepreneurs can understand. The book is structured to take the reader through a progression of understanding what business plans are and what type of plan is best suited for various purposes like planning financials, marketing processes, and operations, and explains different plans for different types of organizations. The content is an excellent source of information that can be used either in introductory entrepreneurship courses or by self-studying professionals.

– Dr. Richard J. Tarpey, Assistant Professor, Jones College of Business

The book does an excellent job of covering the content material for a startup company and including sections for different types of business from service to manufacturing firms. This book would be appropriate for a startup company, a class in Entrepreneurship/Innovation, and a supplement for a Strategic Management capstone course. The format of the book is well-designed with readable pages in an appropriate font size that makes the content per page easier to understand. In my opinion, the Vibrant Self-Learning Management series is one of the best available for gaining applicable knowledge in focused management areas.

– Dr. W. Kevin Baker, Professor of Business Administration, Roanoke College

What experts say about this book!

The World of Business and Entrepreneurship has changed quite a bit since the beginning of the pandemic, but the technicalities of a well-thought-through business plan have remained unchanged! This well-written, well-conceptualized, and easy-to-read book will give you immediate access to all the necessities of writing and understanding a business plan. Many writers have come before, but the authors of this current volume have captured the main themes so elegantly and so practically that each element and detail make so much sense. I commend the authors for this herculean task and invite interested readers to take good note of this wonderful book. A true gem!

– Dr. Franco Gandolfi, (Adjunct) Full Professor,
McDonough School of Business, Washington DC

Business Plan Essentials is a valuable resource for multiple audiences ranging from college students to entrepreneurial startup founders to current small business operators who want to expand their business. Using easy-to-understand terminology, the book covers the basic concepts of conducting the research necessary to create a comprehensive business plan and then explains how to write and edit the plan that will help a business accomplish its objectives. A particularly useful tool is the book's demonstration of business plans for specific situations, such as the service sector, the manufacturing sector, and the nonprofit sector. The book successfully navigates the tricky balance of being comprehensive without overloading the reader. It would be a useful resource in multiple college courses including Introduction to Business, Entrepreneurship, and Nonprofit Management.

– Kurt Stanberry, MBA/JD, Professor of Business Law,
University of Houston Downtown

What experts say about this book!

This book is essential for new entrepreneurs looking to start a business as well as experienced business executives looking to expand into new areas within an existing enterprise. This book not only outlines the key elements of both simple and complex business plans but also offers practical advice on how to create these plans and deliver them with a special outcome in mind. The book leaves the reader feeling they are getting consultation from an expert on how to create a plan for their business.

– David J. Fogarty PhD, MBA.

This book is a thorough "how-to" that would be valuable to entrepreneurs, business students, juniors, and seniors in Management, Marketing, Operations, and Finance classes as it covers all the necessary fundamentals well in a language that is fluid and understandable. The structure, layout, and font of the book are excellent. The publishers did a great job and entrepreneurs and students will find this book a key tool for their pitch.

– Fernando Pargas, Management Professor,
James Madison University

Table of Contents

Preface

A business plan is an important document for various reasons. There are two main objectives for having a business plan: To enable a business owner or a would-be entrepreneur to fully concentrate on some specific areas of their business operations in order to make their business ideas succeed; and, to make it possible for them to achieve both their short-term and long-term ambitions or goals.

As a serious and dedicated entrepreneur, what separates you from those who are just dabbling into business without adequate preparations is equipping yourself with the appropriate amount of knowledge required to navigate your enterprise to success. And a business plan is like a map that a business-minded adventurer needs to carefully and safely journey through the ups and downs of entrepreneurship.

Running a venture is a very difficult task. One of the best approaches to simplifying everything you would do as a business owner is to get a blueprint. That blueprint is your business plan!

You will find Business Plan Essentials to be of invaluable help to you as you begin to prepare or write your business plan. It contains all the necessary information and/or the pieces of advice you would ever need. This book covers all the essential parts of a useful and functional business plan. It will easily guide you through all the required steps in writing and designing a plan that can guarantee you the much-desired efficiency and productivity in business.

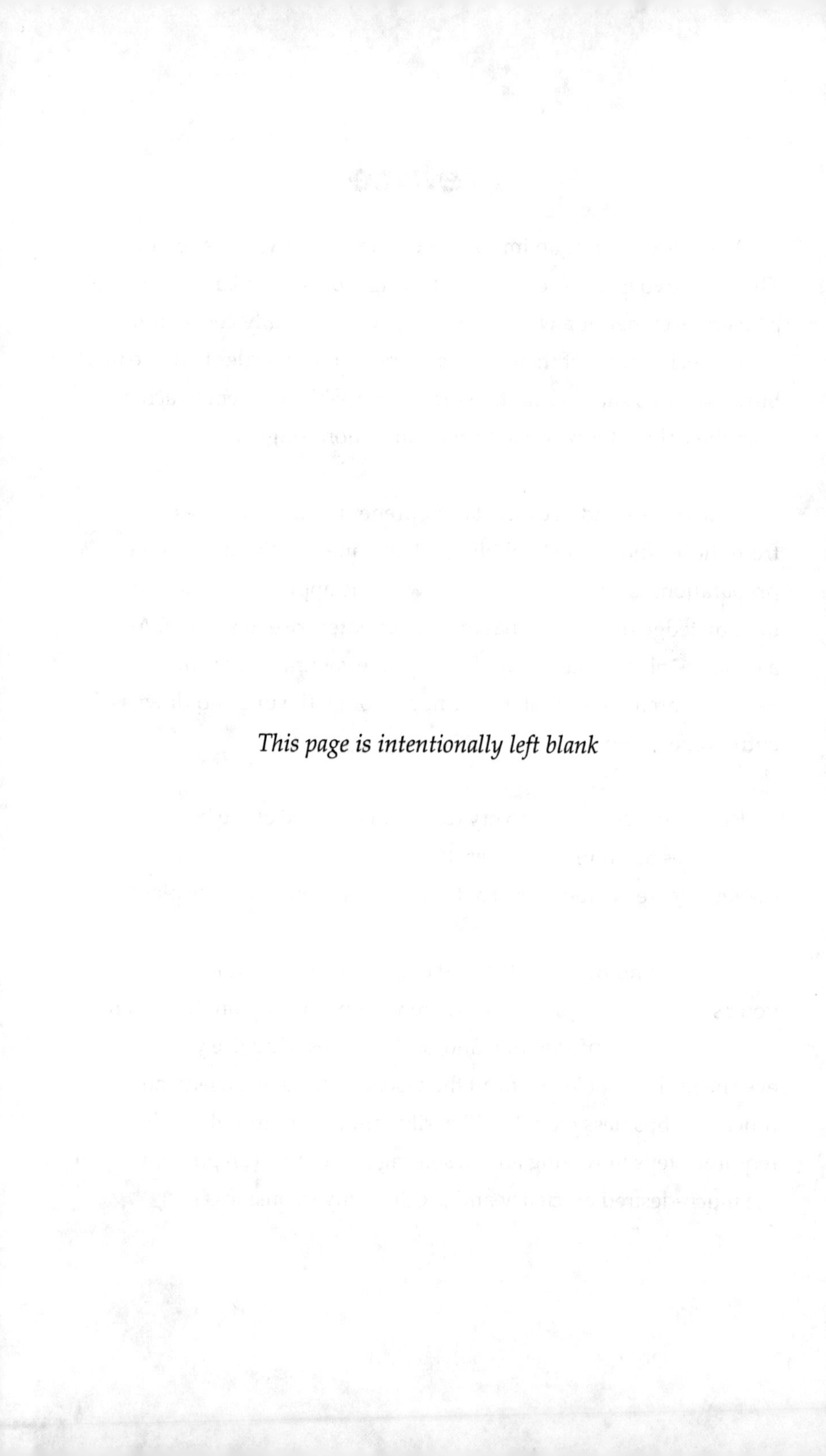

This page is intentionally left blank

Introduction

This is not just another book on how to beautifully craft a business plan, it is indeed "the masterplan" you will need to achieve your impressive purpose of creating a well-designed business plan.

What are your fears? What are the thoughts holding you back from sitting down, creatively outlining your business plan, and eventually writing it to the best of your ability? Different people will respond to these questions differently. It doesn't matter what challenges you may have been facing as you hope to design a useful plan for yourself, this book—Business Plan Essentials—is the only guide that can help you overcome all your fears.

This book will equip you with all the necessary skills you require to produce a high-quality and effective business plan. At the end of this book, you will be able to fully grasp the following concepts that are instrumental to crafting a useful business plan:

- What kind of business plan you need
- Understanding the financials of your proposed or existing business
- Writing your marketing and operational plan
- Performing your marketing analysis
- Writing and editing your business plan

All the above-mentioned attributes of a great business plan are simplified so that you can easily understand and master them.

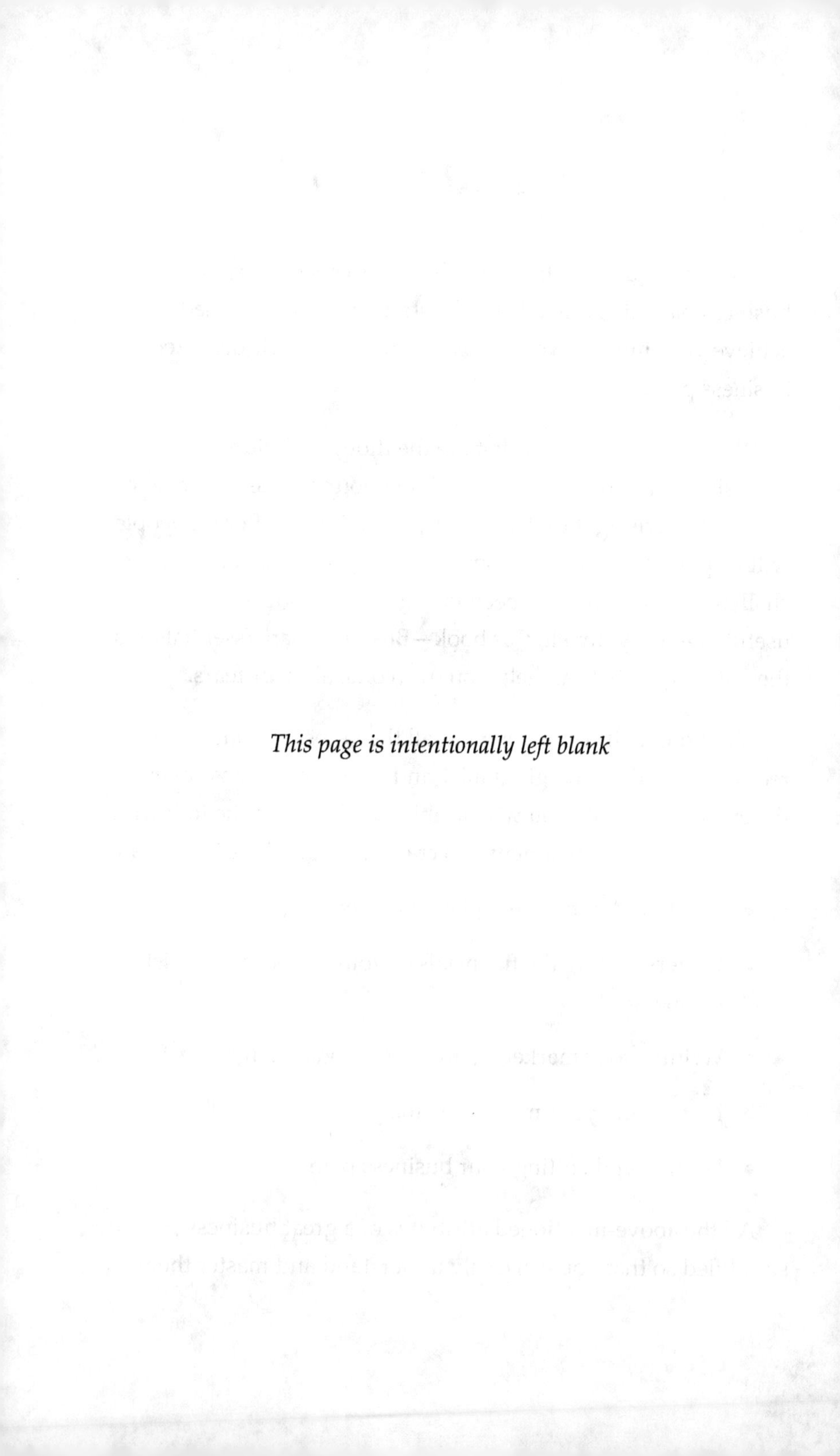

This page is intentionally left blank

Who can benefit from the book?

- A university undergraduate or graduate who has a great idea or concept he/she wants to start a business around.
- An experienced entrepreneur who wants to start a new venture and intends to outline all the required processes to make it happen.
- An owner of an existing business who aspires to revamp or transform it for better performance and profitability by embracing improved methods of running his/her business's day-to-day activities.
- A startup or new business founder(s) who expects to raise funds or money from venture capitalists (VCs). Normally, a VC wants to see the financial and structural strength of a business before they can put their hard-earned money into it.
- The business arm of any research center that hopes to develop products arising from the research that was conducted at a university or independent research laboratory.
- Anyone who desires to run their own business or help others manage their businesses. For instance, when managing a family-owned venture. It may be necessary to restructure an acquired business so as to position it for greater performance.

Whichever way you want to utilize your business plan, the purpose is almost related in all the scenarios. This is because a business plan will reveal a lot of sensitive and important information about the conditions of your business:

- Is it financially sound?
- Is it located in the right place and managed by a group of highly experienced or qualified persons?
- What are the operational processes in place, and how do they contribute to the quality of the products and services that the business will be providing?
- What are the marketing and promotional activities that the business will depend on to expose its products/services to current and prospective customers?

How to use this book?

We write this book as a reference guide for anyone who wants to create a powerful and pragmatic business plan that they can use for either to run their businesses, raise capital/funds for their businesses, or improve operations at their respective enterprises (existing businesses).

In order to derive much practical wisdom from this book, you should:

- **Approach it with an open mind.** You are surely going to discover some new and creative ways to produce a business plan that you can effectively use.
- **Follow each step provided in the book systematically.** It doesn't matter what your business niche or industry is, the procedures highlighted in Business Plan Essentials are applicable to all kinds of businesses. So, get yourself comfortable and explore all the necessary procedures you will need to draft an effective business plan.
- **Take some time to go through some samples of business plans provided in the book.** Even if your business is in another industry, you can still obtain some helpful hints or tips that you can easily utilize for your own benefit.

This page is intentionally left blank

Chapter **1**

Who Needs a Business Plan and for What Purposes?

A business plan can be simply defined as a document that spells out the significant objectives a business aims to achieve in the near future and the strategies it will use to get there. You can consider a business plan to be a viable blueprint the business will utilize to carry out all the necessary activities required to make a product or provide a service, market the product/service, and keep a tab on its finances. It is clear from the onset that any business that wants to remain competitive must have a business plan. As a boat needs a paddle to navigate the currents of the waters, every business requires a business plan to weather all the challenges entrepreneurs will confront while managing their ventures.

Key learning objectives should include the readers' understanding of the following:

- Why Write A Business Plan?

- What Kind of Business Plan Do You Need?
- Do You Know Your Business Pretty Well?
- Getting Started

1.1 Why Write a Business Plan

In his book, ***The Entrepreneur's Manual,*** Richard M. White asserts that "business plans" should be viewed as the "road maps" for creating businesses. He further explains that "you identify your origin, select a destination, and plot the shortest distance between the two points."

As a matter of fact, a business plan helps its authors achieve these three significant objectives:

- A business plan highlights the necessary activities required to successfully establish and manage a business. A detailed business plan should contain sufficient information about the proposed business' goods/services, the available market for those goods or services, and the management style adopted in running the business.
- A business plan can become a yardstick for measuring the progress of a business, identifying if the expected goals and objectives of the business have been accomplished.
- A business plan is used as an essential tool for raising capital from investors as well as obtaining much-needed loans from banks and other financial institutions.

This brings us to the most important question: Who actually needs a business plan? In addition to a business owner or a would-be entrepreneur, it is a common practice for investors, existing companies, and research institutes that have partnerships with the private sector to have a business plan in place.

For any business plan to be effective and serve the purpose for which it was created for, it must answer the following top 10 questions:

- **What is the need that the business will fill or satisfy?** The business you are managing may be a startup or an existing business that has been in operation for several years.
- **How will the business carry out all its functions?** Every business adopts different and unique operational approaches that best suit its objectives. For instance, a manufacturing company will implement policies and procedures that may lead to greater performance in all its business activities. Of course, the manufacturing company's approaches will be different from those utilized by a small store selling second-hand clothes.
- **How will the business differentiate itself from others in the same niche or industry?** Branding should be an integral aspect of your business planning. In other words, you are going to give your business a typical image or reputation that both customers and employees will be very proud of.
- **Who will be the key players in managing the affairs of the business?** It is generally believed that a business is as good as the caliber of people that manage it. And the key executives and managers of your business must be clearly stated in your business plan.

- **How big is the market the business is entering into?** The primary purpose of conducting market research is to investigate how big and lucrative is the market that a business wants to serve. It is through market analysis that the business owner can identify how best to reach out to the customers in that particular market.

- **Who will be the main customers targeted by the business?** Customer identification and segmentation are two mutually intertwined processes that every business should undertake. It pays to know which customers to offer useful products and services to and where they are located, as well as their spending nature or habits.

- **Which effective and promotional strategies will the business utilize to market its products and services?** No business survives on its own—as a business owner, you must present your company and its products/services to the world. And you can mostly accomplish this through effective promotions or marketing.

- **What do the financial statements of the business look like?** Is your business financially strong? How much will it take to successfully run your operations? Is your business able to make enough money in the first, second, or even the third year of its operations to break even?

- **How much startup capital will be required and how will the business be financed before it begins to generate revenues?** If you are going to raise money from outside investors, as a business owner, you would be asked to offer detailed explanations about your business' funding method. Will you be running the business initially from out-of-pocket expenses or obtaining financial assistance from friends, partners, and acquaintances?

- **What is the breakeven point?** How soon will it take for your business to be making money?

1.2 What Kind of Business Plan Do You Need?

There are four unique types of business plans, depending on a particular business owner's needs:

1. **Very short business plans (or mini-plans):** You need a mini business plan if you are self-employed or running a really small business like a pop-and-mum venture. Your small business doesn't necessarily require elaborate operational processes as you serve only a few clients or customers. A typical mini business plan may have about 5-7 questions that you should answer in order to give a specific direction to your business. All your responses to those important questions can occupy just a page.

Figure 1.1 **A sample of mini business plan**

SMALL BUSINESS PLAN

NAME OF COMPANY:____________________

ADDRESS OF COMPANY:____________________

CONTACT PERSON:____________________ TELEPHONE NO.:__________

SBA STATEMENT ON REPRESENTATIVES AND FEES

You are not required to use a representative to complete this business plan. If you chose to hire purpose, the following information must be provided:

Name of Representatives and Addresses	Description of Services	Hourly Rate	Amount Paid

Source: A sample of a mini business plan, by Betty Parks https://www.pinterest.com/pin/sample-small-business-plan-within-sba-business-plan-template-pdf--862228291151392644/

As shown in Fig 1.1, you are only required to enter a little information into the blanks on a single page, which is enough to let others know everything about your business activities. There is no need to state your detailed marketing or financial processes on the business plan.

Other uses of a mini business plan include:

- **Business introduction:** You can introduce your business to angel or unsophisticated investors who may not demand to see the full scope of your business activities and financial standing. Examples of these unsophisticated investors include your friends, colleagues, families, or acquaintances. The sparse information on a mini business plan is enough to convince them that you do have a business that is worth investing in.
- **Onboarding a business development team/consultant:** When looking for a business development consultant, your mini business plan itself may be the necessary document you need to brainstorm with your business development team who will, in turn, advise you about how to best design your full-scale business plan.

2. **Presentation plans or decks:** A presentation business plan, which is also popularly referred to as a presentation deck or simply a pitch deck, is an entirely different tool on its own. A deck is primarily used when pitching to an investor, a financial institution, and even to a prospective, prominent customer. Your deck should be self-explanatory in a way that a potential investor can quickly grasp what benefits people stand to gain from using your products/services and how it is going to make money for the investors through the analysis of its revenue projection. On most occasions, investors do not have a lot of time to sit down and listen to your pitch; hence, your deck should be short, possibly consisting of 10-20 PowerPoint slides that you can reel off within 20-30 minutes. A good pitch deck must contain relevant statistics. Nowadays, you can entirely design a deck using a combination of images, charts, timelines, tables, and very few words. The best practice is to "show"

with a deck and not to "tell"; let the investors make their own informed decisions based on the facts and figures you have presented to them in your deck.

A large percentage of presentation plans or decks nowadays contain fewer words but are filled with graphics that distinctly explain what a business is doing and other necessary facts that must be communicated to investors or future partners.

3. **Working or operational business plans:** When people talk about "a business plan", they are actually referring to the working or operational business plan. It comprises every step that a business needs to proceed from inception into its first three years of management. It is so detail-oriented that a typical operational business plan can be anywhere between 30 and 100 pages, depending on the size of your business and the complexity of your business operations. You are expected to provide adequate information about your business' products/services, operations, marketing and sales strategies, management team, finances, and other related facts. A working business plan is like a "playbook" that a business owner always consults while running his/her business activities. You will need to make sure that you are not outspending your previously budgeted startup expenses, and that you can also strictly follow your predetermined marketing and sales procedures. So, writing a great operational business plan requires time, applicable skills, and experience.

4. **What-if or recovery business plans:** Managing a business is one of the riskiest things to do. According to Investopedia, research shows that 20% of startups fail in the first year. The rate is even higher in the later years as 50% of new businesses

collapse in their fifth year, and 67% in their tenth year.[1] As a business owner, you are contending with many challenges to sail your business to safety. Occasionally, unexpected circumstances beyond your power may occur, like a pandemic, and this will definitely threaten the survival of your business. This is why it is advisable for businesses to put in place "what-if" or "recovery" business plans. This kind of business plan is used to help businesses escape natural or man-made disasters that may force them to fold up. A recovery business plan contains all the necessary emergency steps to be taken to salvage any business that is going through a tough time. It is possible for a business to draft a recovery plan for some of its departments that are not performing well. This document will be used to revamp the business and restructure some business activities that may be dragging the business towards its early demise.

A recovery or well-written contingency plan has five unique purposes for any business that wants to thrive post-emergency or post-disaster:

- **Time- and money-saving:** To kick-start a business after a period of a debilitating pandemic, natural, or artificial disaster, a business can quickly draft a recovery plan and then work assiduously on achieving every step indicated in the plan. This will save such a goal-oriented business time and money. Why? The fact is that many businesses that are currently operating don't have in place a recovery plan they can quickly fall back on when a disaster strikes. The danger is that the longer it takes a business to bounce back after a disaster, the harder it will be for such a company to

1. The 4 Most Common Reasons a Small Business Fails. Retrieved on April 25, 2022 from Investopedia, https://www.investopedia.com/articles/personal-finance/120815/4-most-common-reasons-small-business-fails.asp

maintain its lead in the market or get its previous customers back. It won't take long for such a business to partially suspend all its operations or even collapse immediately. Time, as they say, is money. It is clear that a business has a lot of money to lose if it can't quickly bring itself back after a pandemic or an emergency that has virtually disrupted its smooth business processes.

- **Damage minimization:** With a great recovery plan, a company can systematically minimize the damage done to its business activities by an unavoidable disaster. When a business takes too long to resume operations after a sudden hiatus, it may have to deal with plenty of losses. Its equipment may rust or some perishable raw materials may eventually be wasted. Technically, a business has a lot to gain by drafting a recovery plan even before it doesn't face any challenges that may make it very difficult to manage its day-to-day processes.

- **Quick recovery:** No doubt, a recovery or contingency plan will help a business that has been affected by a pandemic or some kind of emergency to quickly bounce back. In other words, its recovery will be quite quicker than other businesses that do not have contingency plans.

- **Life-saving:** Employees of a business with a good recovery plan can quickly return to their work after the disaster. They will be able to make enough money to look after their families and save themselves and their loved ones from starvation.

- **Reputation-building:** When a business can swiftly get back to operations after a serious emergency, it is not only its employees that will be happy. Even the customers and partners will be glad to see it back in business without much hassle. This will help the business build a respected image for itself. People can rest assured that no matter what happens, the business will be able to supply them with the products/services that they have signed up for.

1.3 Do You Know Your Business Pretty Well?

It is almost impossible for you to prepare an effective business plan if you do not know your business pretty well. It is essential that you understand all the intricacies of your business activities before sitting down to draft a business plan to run it.

Some of the important aspects of your business operations that you should be conversant with include but are not limited to the following:

- **Industry-Wide Experience:** It is helpful if an entrepreneur has some pragmatic experience in the industry he/she is designing a business plan for. No one expects you to be an expert in all areas of your business operations, but it pays to know what exactly you are doing and why you are setting up a business in that industry. In essence, having an idea of the prevailing conditions of the industry, the existing standards and ethics, and the economics of the industry can go a long way to preparing better for the task ahead. Running a business is a difficult but doable task.
- **The Market:** Which segments of the market are you targeting? What demographics do your future clients/ customers belong to? Are you able to offer them what they want and keep them satisfied with your products/services? If you want to be successful as a business owner, it is

imperative that you have a clear understanding of who your customers are and how best to serve them.

- **The Financial Statements:** Starting a business can be likened to erecting a building. From the onset, you must have all the necessary materials needed to complete the edifice. Money is a significant factor in successfully managing a business. So, it is important that you have deep knowledge of your financial preparedness to run a business. How much initial startup capital do you need? What are your projected revenues? How do you plan to make sure that your business consistently makes money? How do you plan to raise money if you do not have enough capital to foot all the necessary bills incurred while managing your business?

- **The Team:** Who are you putting on your team? Are they qualified for the task at hand and will they do a wonderful job? If you are planning to raise money from investors to run your business, you must make sure your team comprises of experienced and versatile professionals who can join hands with you in steering your business towards astounding success.

- **Marketing and Sales:** How would get your products/ services in front of the right customers who need them the most? You need to outline the best marketing and sales strategies that you will adopt to manage the affairs of your business.

- **Products/Services:** The most sensitive aspect of knowing your business has to do with your products and services. Are the products you are offering your customers good enough to help them solve their existing problems or pain points? Will they be willing to pay a fair price for deriving maximum benefits from your products/services? What differentiates your products and services from the others in the marketplace?

1.4 Getting Started

Drafting a business plan is not rocket science; it is something you can do if you are well prepared for it. Whether you are a newbie entrepreneur or an experienced business owner, you should approach writing your business plan with absolute seriousness.

Here are three fundamental steps you can take to develop a very useful business plan for your venture:

- **Choosing the type of business plan that you perfectly need:** You have discovered in this chapter that there are four unique kinds of business plans employed for different purposes. To save time and money, you should only go for the type that will best serve the purpose that you need it for. It is not sensible to spend money preparing a 50-page business when all you need is a 10-slide pitching deck.
- **Gathering the appropriate documents:** Businesses that have been in existence for some years already have data from which you can obtain vital information to prepare your business plan. On the other hand, a newly established startup may have no historical data to draw conclusions from. In that case, you can obtain some ideas from a related business that has the same size and concept as yours. In this situation, most of the content in your business plan will be projections---projected expenses, sales, revenues, and profits.

- **Sitting down to draft your business plan:** After gathering all the necessary information that will go into your business plan, you still need to put them down in black and white. If you are not good at business writing, you may want to hire a freelance copywriter to help you.

Discussion Questions

1. What do you think is the most sensitive part of writing a business plan?

2. Is it possible for someone who doesn't know his/her business well to design an effective business plan for it?

3. What are the three steps everyone should take while getting ready to draft their business plan?

Quiz

1. **If you are pitching to investors, which is the most appropriate business plan to use?**
    a. Mini plan
    b. Presentation deck
    c. Recovery plan

2. **A Business plan is not used for:**
    a. Renting a permanent office for the business
    b. Monitoring the progress of the business year-on-year
    c. Setting out a definite plan of action for running a business

3. **.......is a document that business owners use to describe their products/services, how their products are made, their financial statements, marketing and sales strategies, and the business management.**
    a. A business plan
    b. A contract
    c. A voucher

4. **A typical operational business plan ranges from ......pages.**
    a. 5 to 10
    b. 30 to 100
    c. 1 to 5

5. **How many presentation slides should an ideal pitch deck have?**

   a. Anywhere from 10 to 20 slides

   b. More than 50 slides

   c. 100 slides

6. **What is the best method for preparing the financials for a new business?**

   a. By the use of projections

   b. By borrowing data from another business

   c. It is not important to have the financials of a business plan

7. **Why is it important to have a section of the business plan showing how the organization is managed?**

   a. To showcase the qualifications of the team

   b. To brag about the experience of the team to investors

   c. To make customers happy

8. **All but one of these documents is helpful in preparing the financials of an existing business.**

   a. Receipts

   b. Bank statements/tellers

   c. Business owner's picture

9. How difficult is it to draft a business plan?

a. Very difficult

b. Anyone who understands the fundamentals of a business plan can write one.

c. I don't know

10. Knowing your business very well entails that you should have a clear idea about your business's.....

a. industry and market

b. products/services

c. physical office

Answers					
	1 – b	2 – a	3 – a	4 – b	5 – a
	6 – a	7 – a	8 – c	9 – b	10 – a

Chapter Summary

- It is fair to say that every business needs a business plan, but there are four unique kinds of business plans they can choose from.
- As a blueprint, a business plan can guide a business owner through the murky waters of entrepreneurship.
- Before preparing a workable business plan, an entrepreneur should have a functional knowledge of the business he/she wants to establish.
- It has become the norm nowadays that any business owner who aspires to raise money from outside investors must have a business plan in hand.
- A new business that doesn't have historical data that could be used to draft the business plan can rely on future projections as far as its financial reports are concerned.

References

- Bryant, S. (2020). "How many startups fail and why?" *Investopedia. https://www.investopedia.com/articles/personal-finance/040915/how-many-startups-fail-and-why.asp#:~:text=Research%20concludes%2021.5%25%20of%20startups%20fail%20in%20the,and%20not%20being%20an%20expert%20in%20the%20industry.*

- Horton, M. (2022). "The 4 most common reasons a small business fails." *Investopedia. https://www.investopedia.com/articles/personal-finance/120815/4-most-common-reasons-small-business-fails.asp*

- White, Richard M. (2014). *The Entrepreneur's Manual: Business Start-Ups, Spin-Offs, and Innovative Management.* Kent: Churchill and Dunn Ltd.

Chapter 2

Understanding the Financials of Your Proposed or Existing Business

Money is as important to any business as blood is to human bodies. Without a solid financial foundation or lifeline, a business is doomed to fail right from its first of day establishment. Hence, it is now a common practice for startup founders to embrace financial literacy. To succeed in the difficult terrain of entrepreneurship, you must regularly "know your numbers!" This entails a deep understanding of your business's financial health. One of the best approaches to having a full grasp of your business's financials is through budgeting. Budgeting affords business owners the opportunity to perpetually appraise their financial strengths, knowing how much they have in their balances, how they would need to run their businesses, and what methods to employ in raising money to cover up the shortfalls in their financial expectations.

Therefore, to prepare a good business plan, you must sink your teeth into your business' numbers. You should have an understanding of how much your products/services are priced, how much you could make, and how to spend your revenues in managing the day-to-day affairs of your venture.

Key learning objectives include the readers' understanding of the following:

- Budgeting for Startup Expenses
- Estimating Prices and Projecting Sales Volumes
- Forecasting Your Average Cost of Sales and Profit and Loss
- Preparing Your Cash Flow Forecast
- Ways to Raise Money

2.1 Budgeting for Startup Expenses

Startup budgeting is an essential part of all business plans. When starting a business, there are some compulsory expenses you have to make to get things rolling. However, these expenses may differ from one industry to another. Highlighted below are a number of mandatory or necessary expenses every would-be business owner must pay attention to..

- **Consultancy fees:** If you are undecided whether to buy a business or start one from scratch, you may need to seek some advice from business consultants or business development experts. You may be charged per hour or per project as you utilize their services to help you make the right decision about how to pursue your entrepreneurship ambitions.

- **Business registration:** With the exception of mom-and-pop businesses, it is always advisable to register your business. This will give you a head start over others in branding and unique proposition. Depending on the nature of your business, it can be registered as a sole proprietorship, partnership, or limited liability company. In the United States, businesses are normally registered.

- **Physical facility:** When you need physical facilities such as an office, store, or other fixed assets to run your business, you will be asked to pay for these at the beginning of your operations. So, it is important that you budget for it, or else you may have no place to run your business. Even for online businesses like e-commerce and online learning institutions, you need to physically ship some of your products to your customers. In this case, you will be expected to invest in a fulfillment process.

- **Hiring employees:** A small business may need some extra hands for smooth operation, which means that you may want to hire 2-5 employees to support you in your entrepreneurship drive. A medium-sized enterprise would require at least 10-15 workers to stay operational. And hiring, training, and onboarding employees costs money.

- **Advertising/marketing:** It is imperative for businesses to advertise or promote their products/services to both their existing and prospective customers to stay in business. Even in this age of digital marketing, it still costs a sizeable amount of money to run successful marketing campaigns.

- **Suppliers:** If you are in retail and your business depends largely on reselling other businesses' products/services, you may need to set aside some funds to pay your suppliers, without whom it may be difficult to maintain your business model.

All these expenses could add up to a substantial amount of money considering that there are 12 months in a year and some of these expenses are recurring monthly expenses. However, bear in mind that for your business to be in operation and make money, you can never shy away from the above-stated expenditures. This is why they must be clearly indicated in your business plan so that you can know exactly what you are getting yourself into. Your investors will also appreciate that you have clearly input these expenses in your business plan so that they know the extent of help you need to get your business running and to decide whether they are good investors for your business or not.

Sometimes, new business owners suffer headaches in planning their proposed business budgets appropriately. It is a common problem faced by new entrepreneurs, so, if you are one of them, you shouldn't fret at all about this issue. You have two options at your disposal: You could hire a financial expert to help you do the budgeting correctly, or you may learn how to do it yourself.

If you choose to do it yourself, these budgeting strategies may be of immense help to you:

- **Investigate the budgeting standards in the industry:** Take, for instance, that you are planning to open a restaurant in New York or London or Mumbai. You may need to investigate how much it will cost you in that particular location. You will discover the final budgeting that is not far from the exact amount you will need to run the restaurant in your chosen location.

- **Use a spreadsheet:** You can simplify your budgeting process by making use of a spreadsheet. You may be required to learn and master some simple spreadsheet computations, though, to easily identify and interpret your business' numbers on a spreadsheet. Divide your accounts into "marked or named" columns so that you can quickly find them whenever you want to do some business expense calculations.
- **Work with someone:** You may be lucky to have someone good at numbers to assist you in conducting your business's budgeting. The person could be your prospective business partner, an associate, or even a dependable family member. They will be able to help you balance all those accounts you are struggling with. The bottom line is that you have an accurate estimate of what it would cost to run your business operations, especially at the earliest stage of establishing your enterprise.

2.2 Estimating Prices and Projecting Sales Volumes

One of the important actions you will take in ensuring that your startup financials are in good order is to estimate the price your products/services will be sold for.

There are four approaches you can use to calculate how much your prospective customers will be asked to pay for using your products/services:

- **Cost-oriented pricing:** You should factor in the cost of making your products before deciding on their final prices. There are two ways to do this—you can either markup the price of the products after deducting the cost of producing them or apply break-even pricing to them. In the case of markup pricing, you are increasing the price of your products based on the average price of the same product sold in the marketplace. For instance, a toothbrush costs $1 to manufacture. If the selling price of related toothbrushes in the market are $4 - $5 per toothbrush, you can markup your price to at least $4 to remain competitive in the market. However, for break-even pricing, you are just barely recouping the cost of making the product with very little profit. Some products are costly to make, so in that situation, you may opt for a break-even pricing system just to make a small profit but have the products available for your customers. Suppose it costs you $52 to make a pair of flip-flops, but the average price of flip-flops is $55. Instead of marking up the price to say $60 or $70, you may want to settle for the average price of the product in the market, which is $55. This reveals that you are barely breaking even with a $3 profit.

- **Competition-oriented pricing:** As the name implies, with a competition-oriented pricing system, you are compelled to price your products/services the same as your competitors' or even slightly lower than theirs so that you are able to find buyers for your products. Normally, consumers won't be interested in products that are too expensive when they can find good alternatives in the market. So, if your competitors are selling their products for a price that ranges from $30 to $45, you may want to stay in the middle and offer yours for $35.

- **Demand-oriented pricing:** When there is a huge demand for your products and little supply of them in the marketplace, this affords you a unique opportunity to markup your price as you want because there are consumers who are willing to pay any amount of money to get what they need at that particular time.
- **Market-oriented pricing:** This method of pricing strictly follows the common price regime in the market. In other words, you are selling your products for exactly how much consumers are willing to pay for them. It is understandable that very few consumers will be interested in buying $200-worth of bread when the average price of bread in the market is between $5 and $10. So, sometimes, the market can dictate how to price products/services. It is not sensible to overprice your products with the hope that consumers will still purchase them. Such overpriced commodities will end up being stacked or stored up as inventories for a long period of time, without being sold.

Once you have reasonably priced your products/services, you can now go ahead with projecting the sales volumes for your products/services. You will need this figure to precisely project the revenues for your business, which you are going to input into your business plan.

Highlighted below are three reliable models for accurately predicting sales volumes:

- **Qualitative Techniques:** You can utilize this model to predict the sale volumes of your products if you do not have enough sales data to project how many products will the consumers be purchasing at a particular period of time. This model relies heavily on human judgment and rating systems. In short, if you do not fully understand your penetration and market acceptance rates, this model can give you a good estimation of how your products will perform in the marketplace. Qualitative techniques entail using surveys and questionnaires to gauge buyers' expectations. It also adopts the use of market research and sales personnel's forecasts to calculate the volume of products that will be sold per month, quarter, or any other period within a fiscal year. In other words, you simply need to investigate your prospective customers' interests or needs and convert that information into data that could be used to predict their future buying behaviors.

- **Time Series Analysis:** This model is quite useful when you have already obtained some sales data about a product or a product line. You can perform an analysis of the available data to predict how consumers will interact with the same products in the near future. For example, if you have been selling sweaters in winter for the past five years, you now have some data that could reveal a lot about your customers' behaviors: you know where the most loyal customers are, their demographics, when they are likely to purchase your sweaters, and which pricing works well for them. With this method, you can have a distinct picture of how your product will perform in the market when winter comes.

- **Causal models:** What makes this model different from the first two techniques is that it is a sales forecasting method that requires a lot of historical sales data. In essence, while it is possible to use the Time Series Analysis Model with data collected over a year or two, the Causal model will however require data gathered for over 5 to 15 years. Without a doubt, the Causal Model offers the most convincing result when it comes to exactly predicting sales volumes for a business.

If your business has been in existence for some time, it is advisable that you utilize either the Time Series Analysis model or the Causal Model while estimating sales volumes for a specific period of time. If your business is a startup with little or no sales data, the best approach for estimating the number of your future sales is through the Qualitative Technique.

Whichever approach you choose to use, the goal is to accurately predict your business' performance in the marketplace in terms of how many products it will be able to sell within a specific period of time.

2.3 Forecasting Your Average Cost of Sales and Profit and Loss

You don't have to be an accountant or a bookkeeper to precisely forecast your average cost of sales and profit and loss. However, they should be accurate enough to reveal the true nature of your business's financial health to prospective investors and possible partners.

You can use the following formulas to calculate your average cost of sales and profit and loss model:

Cost of Sales

Cost of sales, which is also known as cost of goods sold (COGS), is defined as the total amount it takes for a business to manufacture and sell a product. All operating businesses must track these useful metrics and periodically estimate their costs of sales.

For instance, a company that had an inventory worth $100,000 at the beginning of the year spent another $50,000 to purchase some much-needed raw materials while spending $40,000 on labor and $50,000 on manufacturing. The company ended the year with an inventory estimated to be $10,000. What is the cost of sales for the company's products in the year under review?

The formula for calculating the cost of sales is provided below:

Cost of Sales = Beginning inventory + Raw material purchases + Cost of direct labor + Overhead manufacturing cost – Ending inventory

Using the formula to estimate the cost of goods sold for the company in the example,

Cost of Sales = $100,000 +$50,000 +$40,000 + $50,000 - $10,000 =$230,000

Therefore, the company incurred $230,000 as its cost of sales during the year under calculation.

For a startup, the values for the beginning and ending inventories can be roughly or approximately estimated based on the previously projected sales volumes, as shown above.

Profit/Loss model

An integral part of the financials of your existing or new business, which is required to be input into your business plan is the profit/loss model. It includes important information that prospective investors or partners will be eager to check out in your business plan.

A business's profit or loss can easily be calculated with this simple formula:

Profit/Loss = Income- Expenses

For instance, if your business income is $100,000 and your expenses for the same period under calculation is $30,000, then:

Profit = $100,000 - $30,000 = $70,000

There are two types of profits in accounting: Gross Profit and Net Profit.

Gross Profit = Sales– Cost of Sales (or cost of goods sold)

Net Profit = Gross profit- Expenses

However, your existing or new business may incur losses if its expenses are more than its income, as demonstrated below:

If your business spends $80,000 while its revenues are $20,000 during the same period, your business' losses can be estimated thus:

Loss = $80,000 - $20,000 = $60,000

NOTE: It must be stated that for medium-sized or large-sized businesses, you will need to prepare your business's actual or projected income statement or report to be able to accurately estimate your business' profit/loss model.

An **income statement** is a financial document that lists all the incomes and expenses your business makes during a period, which could be a month, a quarter, or a year.

Some of the income entries on a typical income statement include:

- The Sale of Services
- The Sale of Products
- Funds from other incomes such as interest earned on savings at the bank

The record for your business's expenses should contain information only about deductible expenses, which include:

- Accounting Expenses
- Amortization
- Audit Costs
- Advertising
- Bookkeeping Fees
- Bank Charges
- Cleaning
- Computer Expenses
- Consultation Fees
- Discounts Given
- Discounts Taken
- Employee Expenses
- Entertainment Expenses
- Equipment Rent
- Freight and Delivery Charges
- Insurance
- Interest Expense (e.g. interest paid on a loan or bank overdraft)
- Internet/Web Hosting
- Motor Vehicle Expenses (such as fuel and repairs)
- Office Supplies
- Promotions
- Stationery
- Rent
- Pension Expense
- Power
- Printing and Photocopying
- Professional Development
- Repairs and Maintenance

- Staff Amenities
- Subscriptions
- Telephone
- Small Tools and Equipment
- Travel and Accommodation
- Wages, Salaries and Bonuses

You cannot include non-deductible expenses listed below in your profit and loss statements. Hence, they should be included when calculating your overall expenses:

- Interests on loan repayments
- Inventory
- Taxes
- Owner's Drawings
- Investments

2.4 Preparing Your Cash Flow Forecast

Cash flow is king in any business. In other words, if your business doesn't have a good cash flow, it will soon lack adequate financial resources to run its day-to-day business activities. In dire circumstances, your business can go bankrupt if it cannot make as much money as it requires to stay afloat and thrive.

Cash flow (CF) can simply be defined as the increase or decrease in the amount of money a business, an individual, or an organization has at a given period of time.

There are three types of cash flows:

- **Cash flow from operational activities:** A business may be able to stay liquid owing to some smooth infusion of cash from its operational activities. For example, it will produce certain products, sell them, and reinvest the money into the business. This cycle can facilitate the business's operations since it has enough financial resources to manage its activities.
- **Cash flow from financial activities:** A business can receive a financial lifeline from banks and other financial institutions to maintain its operations without any disruption.
- **Cash flow from investing activities:** It is also possible for a business to make enough money from investing in another company. This investing process, if profitable, will help keep money in the business.
- **Break-even point:** This is the point when the business starts making a profit. So, if it took $1000 to start the business, and the service or product was sold at $50 each, with an overhead cost of $500, the break-even point will occur in Month 4:

Table 2.1

Income		Product price ($)	Month 1	Month 2	Month 3	Month 4	Month 5
Total Income		50	$500.00	$750.00	$1,000.00	**$1,500.00**	$2,000.00
Expenses							
Fixed expenses/ Startup capital	$1,000						
Total expenses			$500.00	$500.00	$500.00	**$500.00**	$500.00
Net Profit			$ -	$250.00	$500.00	**$1,000.00**	$1,500.00
Total balance			$(1,000.00)	$(750.00)	$(500.00)	$ -	$500.00

Figure 2.1 Breakeven Point Chart

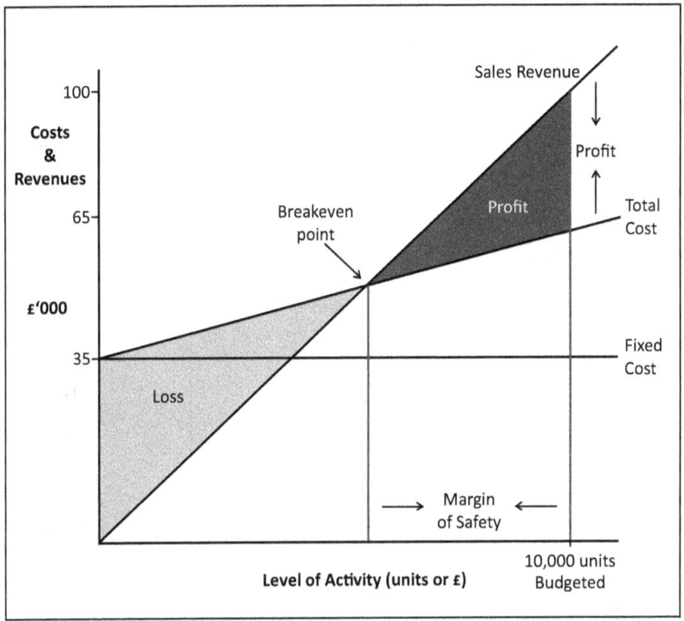

Source: This chart above is from SaPartners
https://sapartners.com/lean-finance/leanfinancebreakevenchart/

It is very easy to estimate the cash flow for an existing business, especially the one that has been in operation for 2 to 5 years. On the other hand, a cash flow statement for a newly established business can only be drawn from forecasting or projection.

Figure 2.2 **A sample Cash flow statement**

Cash Flow Statement Company XYZ **FY Ended 31 Dec 2017** All Figures in USD		
Cash Flow From Operations		
Net Earnings		2,000000
Additions to Cash		
Depreciations Decrease in Accounts Receivable Increase in Accounts Payable Increase in Taxes Payable		10,000 15,000 15,000 2,000
Subtractions From Cash		
Increase in Inventory		(30,000)
Net Cash From Operations		2,012,000
Cash Flow From Investing		
Equipment		(500,000)
Cash Flow From Financing		
Notes Payable		10,000
Cash Flow for FY Ended 21 Dec 2017		**1,522,000**

Source: A cash flow sample (Investopedia) https://www.investopedia.com/investing/what-is-a-cash-flow-statement/

A very important part of cash flow is knowing how much money there is to operate.

If you sell 10 items per week for $10 and have a gross profit of $100 per week, and the cost of goods sold is $7 each, you net a profit of $70 per week. If this goes on for 3 months, you now have $840 in cash. Then you are given an offer to buy your inventory of products (so you do not have to manufacture them) at a cost of $5 each but you must purchase 100 pieces at a time. This means spending $500 of the $840, leaving you with $340. Can you really afford the deal?

Think about how you meet your expenses such as paying employees if there is money tied up in inventory.

If there is an operational budget whereby expenses are met and the number of items sold remains at 10 per week, then this "deal," while it may be appealing, is not fiscally feasible.

The price point, which is what you decide to sell your product or service at, can directly affects your cash flow. You want to be sure not to charge too much over and above what your competitors charge and what the market can bear. In a similar vein you don't want to charge too little and leave yourself short on cash flow.

For medium and large-sized businesses, the idea of cash flow goes beyond how much cash your business has in the bank or in hand. It is all about maintaining a balance between the inflow and outflow of cash. Even a company that is not making any profit can be considered cash flow positive if its business processes and distribution/supply chains are working perfectly and money comes in when it is most needed.

2.5 Ways to Raise Money

It is not an overstatement that most businesses actually prepare their business plans for the singular purpose of getting funding or money for their businesses from investors or partners. So, if down the line you may also show interest in raising some capital to run your business, it is advisable that you should treat this book as an important guide. Everything that is presented here is to help you design the best business plan you could ever make. Investors like business plans that are factual, easy to digest, and well-prepared.

Assuming you are interested in raising some capital for your business, these are six strategic avenues from which you could get some money to run your business activities:

- **Personal contacts:** The first set of people that you can get money from to run your business are your personal contacts. This includes your friends, families, and colleagues. If they like the prospect of your business idea, they will jump on the train with you to make your dreams come true. It is imperative that you also understand that not every friend or family member can add value to the business you are starting or managing. Hence, it will be counterproductive to raise money from them. You should selectively work or collaborate with those that can help you succeed in your entrepreneurship. It is a common fallacy that couples should not co-invest in a business (there are some businesses that are jointly run by husbands and wives that are doing pretty well, but this may be the exception rather than the rule!).

- **Angel investment:** Angels are low-capital net-worth investors who may be willing to assist you in your entrepreneur journey. They can particularly help you with seed investments, which can range from $1000 to about $50,000. However, do not be carried away while getting investors' money and neglect the most important aspect of raising funds. Once you have taken an investor's funds, you are automatically signing him/her up as the co-owner of your business. Unfortunately, people are different and they sometimes come to the table with different perspectives about how to manage a business. To save yourself of all the headaches that may come later from choosing a bad and incompatible investor, you should only collaborate with the angel investors whose aspirations and goals align with yours.

- **Business loans:** If you like, you can decide to go through the traditional way, which is approaching banks and other financial institutions for loans to operate your business. The truth is that it is more difficult to secure a business loan than to obtain funds from families and angel investors. Normally, a financial institution will request collateral from you, which could be your real estate or other landed property. In the absence of qualifiable collaterals, many owners of small and medium-sized businesses have had their hopes dashed from time to time.
- **Crowdfunding:** All hope is not lost. If you have been turned back by banks and other financial institutions, you can still explore the opportunities presented by crowdfunding. This is the latest mass-investment drive made possible by some crowdfunding sites such as Indiegogo, Kickstarter, GoFundMe, Patreon, etc. They allow you to pitch your business idea (with a prototype) to a lot of people that visit their websites. Anyone interested in your idea may pledge some money in return for some favors that may include physical goods or other software products/services.
- **Venture capital:** If you are looking for a large investment to get your business off the ground, your best bet is securing capital from a venture capitalist. Venture capitalists are highly sophisticated and selective investors. If you are fortunate, and your business idea is great, you may get yourself anywhere from $250,000 to even $1 billion or more!

> Venture capital investment is a part of series A to C. Series A financing comes after the seed round—which may include the money obtained from friends, families, and angel investors. The Series A may come from one or two venture capital companies. Series B is usually larger than Series A, and then the final Series is C, which is the largest investment a company may raise before going public or being sold to or merged with another competitor.

NOTE: Here is the most important information you should think about: Apart from your personal contacts and crowdfunding supporters, all the remaining sources of funding for businesses require a well-written and properly designed business plan!

For each stage of external financing invested in your business, your ownership of the business is diluted. In other words, you lose a chunk of your business' equity every time you take money from outside investors. To illustrate this better: you will start with 100% ownership of your business when you are establishing it. This means that the business belongs entirely to you. However, as you take investors aboard, you will have to exchange the equity in your business for the money or funds you are receiving from investors. It is advisable that you work with an experienced investment bank or agency before exposing your business to external financing. If you do not do it properly, you may end up losing your business.

Be careful not to exaggerate the extent of your proposed or existing business's financial strength for the singular purpose of making investors put their hard-earned money into your business. If they later find out that you have been feeding them falsehoods all the while, this may affect their relationship with you. In certain circumstances, angry investors can decide to pull out of investing in your business. Moreover, it is illegal and a treasonable felony to lie and deceive people with the intention of robbing them of their money. Hence, the financial information you will be presenting in your business plan must be exact, genuine, and verifiable.

Discussion Questions

1. What are the four methods of determining a product's or a service's pricing?
2. Is a venture capitalist the best way to raise money for a business in this capitalist age?
3. What are the three strategic approaches for predicting a business' sales volume?

Quiz

1. **Which of the following ways to raise money can provide you with a capital investment as big as $200 million?**
   a. Personal contacts
   b. Angel investors
   c. Venture capitalists

2. **The most accurate approach for predicting a company's sales volume is through.....**
   a. casual models
   b. qualitative techniques
   c. time series analysis

3. **A cash flow positive business is in a great financial position.**
   a. True
   b. False
   c. I don't know

4. **Which of the following cannot be included in your business' profit and loss statement?**
   a. Deductible expenses
   b. Non-deductible expenses
   c. Amortization

5. **These are some cogent reasons for doing startup budgeting except....**

    a. knowing the costs of running the company

    b. discovering if the business needs to raise funds before starting its operations

    c. paying taxes on the business's earnings

6. **One of the following is not the source of cash flow for a business that has already been in operation for 4-5 years.**

    a. Investment

    b. Financial activities

    c. Raising money from personal contacts

7. **All of these are non-deductible expenses except.....**

    a. taxes

    b. depreciation

    c. loan repayments

8. **A company's profit profile can be expressed in two forms, which are.....**

    a. profit and loss

    b. gross profit and net profit

    c. expenses and profit

9. What happens to a business that has more expenses than income?

a. It is running at a loss

b. It is making enough profits

c. I don't know

10. Another name for the sales cost is....

a. cost of goods sold

b. profit margin

c. net investment

Answers	1 – c	2 – a	3 – a	4 – b	5 – c
	6 – c	7 – b	8 – a	9 – a	10 – a

Chapter Summary

- In the absence of a pragmatic budget, it is almost impossible to manage a business without running into difficult problems and headwinds.
- It is advisable that every business must assign a specific price to each of its products/services and project what its sales volume could be in the foreseeable future, in order to be considered profitable by prospective investors or partners.
- To estimate any business's average cost of sales or cost of goods sold, efforts must be deployed towards measuring the applicable metrics such as its inventory, cost of manufacturing, direct labor cost, and raw material expenses.
- A Profit and Loss report or income statement gives a clear picture of how profitable a business is or will be in the near future.
- Without a sustainable cash flow, a business is liable to collapse at any time when it runs out of financial resources to manage its operations.
- A well-designed and clearly presented business plan is required to raise money for a business from sophisticated investors.

References

- Brennan, K. (2019). Startup CFO: The finance handbook for your growing business. Seattle: Amazon.

- Murphy, Chris B. (2022). "Understanding the Cash Flow Statement." *Investopedia. https://www.investopedia.com/investing/what-is-a-cash-flow-statement/*

This page is intentionally left blank

Chapter 3

Writing Your Marketing and Operational Plan

A plan is something you can use as a guide to direct you into making credible decisions and acting sensibly. In this case, a business plan is a guideline that offers clear steps, directions, actions, and processes to follow in order to achieve outstanding performance in your business operations. Without a doubt, a marketing plan and an operational plan are considered to be the two main backbones of any business plan. Not having them in your business will reduce everything you have written in the plan to aimless chit-chat. A marketing plan shows how your business will be promoted or advertised to prospective customers, whereas an operational plan indicates how you hope to satisfactorily serve your customers after winning their hearts through a comprehensive marketing drive. Interestingly enough, both the marketing plan and operational plan go hand-in-hand. No business can survive without them. Imagine how insensible it would feel to open your doors to strangers but fail to entertain them when you had already succeeded in bringing them into your home.

Key learning objectives should include the readers' understanding of the following:

- The Marketing Plan
- The Operational Plan

3.1 Marketing Plan

In your business plan, you must clearly state how you are going to promote your business. Gone are the days when businesses thrive only on word-of-mouth. Instead, you must come up with a well-defined marketing plan that will provide the details of all the necessary steps you are going to take to advertise your products or services.

The following sections must be included in your promotional plan in order to clarify all the marketing practices you want to use to get your products to the consumers that need them:

Key message: It is advisable you have a "key message" you would like to convey to your current or prospective customers. You may want to call this "key message" your business "catchphrase" that everyone can associate with your products/services. For example, most consumers can never forget Nike's "Just Do It", for McDonald's, it is "I'm Lovin' It", and for Tesla, it is "Ride Free". This key message should be inscribed on your business's visuals such as graphics, documents, signs, and other things consumers can see physically.

Owners of small- and medium-sized businesses sometimes fret about how they should phrase the most impactful brand key messages for their businesses. This is a common concern, but you can handle this by concentrating on the following three techniques for crafting a converting and much-loved brand messages:

- **Focusing on who your audience is:** You can save yourself a lot of trouble by giving your targeted customers exactly what they want. Your brand message should reflect that you are intentionally looking after. For instance, Nike empowers its customers, who are mostly athletes, to "Just Do It!" If you are running an educational business, you can inscribe words that are related to learning excellence or getting more wisdom from being educated. You want to show your customers immediately that your business was set up to provide the much-needed solution to their pain points. Realizing that you are looking out for them, they will pay you back by becoming loyal fans or supporters of your business.

- **Have a direct impact on people's emotions:** The easiest way to get noticed by the market you are serving is to use expressions that can rouse the emotions of the people in that market. You want them to feel your care and empathize with your purpose. That is the only way to catch their attention and turn them into supportive customers.

- **Be original and genuine:** It is not sensible to copy an existing brand message because when your customers discover that you are an imitator, they may have a hard time trusting your originality. This is why your key brand message must be unique, new, and reasonable. Such a message will remain in your customers' minds for a very long time to come.

Marketing activities: You should highlight all the necessary marketing activities you will be undertaking to give your business enough visibility in a marketplace that is already crowded with other businesses offering the same products/services like yours. This requires you to list and explain all the promotional options you would be employing to achieve good product recognition, get reliable leads, increase your store traffic, and subsequently convert them into paying customers. Your preferred could be one or a combination of the following promotional processes:

- **Traditional media:** Will you be buying advertising in some traditional media such as radio, magazine, television, newspaper, etc.?
- **Direct mail:** Are you sending direct mails to your prospective customers?
- **Telephone solicitation:** This involves cold-calling your prospective leads in an attempt to turn them into paid customers.
- **Digital marketing:** One of the wonders of the modern age is that you can now advertise your business's products and services on the internet. Will you be using this approach? Social media, email marketing, content marketing, and SEO, for example, are some of the most useful forms of digital marketing.
- **Promotions at business conferences, seminars, and expositions:** Are you thinking of selling your products at business conferences, seminars, workshops, and expositions?

The details provided in your marketing plan can give investors some idea of how your sales strategy will look. This is why it is advisable to provide all the necessary information about your marketing approach in your business plan.

In addition to this, you may want to shed some light on whether you will be hiring full-time commissioned marketing or sales people or you will be using those on contract sales.

The bottom line is that investors will support a business with a well-developed marketing plan. If you are going to grow as a business, you must have a well-defined sales strategy that results in increased sales. In practice, it is the smooth cash flow in your business that will save it from collapsing. If you cannot make enough revenues to run your day-to-day business operations, chances are that you may not be able to attract good investors or partners to your business.

As a result of this, any business plan that has a shoddily prepared marketing plan indicates that the owner of the business does not have what it takes to run a business, as grit in managing a business is mostly needed during marketing or sales promotions.

3.2 Operational Plan

An operational plan is like a guide that provides all the concrete directions or steps required for managing your business. An effective business plan must have a well-written operational plan that includes information on how your business will develop and maintain a loyal customer base. It must also highlight the necessary management responsibilities and capabilities

Some of these topics must be covered in an operational plan to make it convincing enough and reasonable:

Order fulfilment: You need to fully describe your business's processes for making its products and services available to its customers. You should also indicate how you are going to track your customer base, what methods of communications you will use, and how to manage the sales information or data obtained from this interaction. Do you have an existing fulfilment system in place or are you going to be using a third-party fulfilment? What steps are you going to take to make sure that your customers are satisfactorily served or looked after? Does your business have an efficient supply chain that can ship products from your factory to the consumers without any operational hiccups on the way? This information reveals how ready and capable your business is in supplying its products to your customers.

Payment: An integral aspect of your operational plan is your payment methods. How do you want your customer base to pay for the goods and services they are enjoying? In cash, by credit card, or bank transfer? It is essential that you describe the standard payment terms for your business. Would you be willing to allow your customers to pay by installments or you would require an outright payment? Will you be charging any fees for late payment, and if so, at what percentage? It is advisable that you list all the acceptable payment types so that customers can quickly make buying decisions, once having seen that their preferred payment method is okay. On most occasions, customers do not necessarily have the time to cold-call a business to find out if they accept a credit card or cash; it is your responsibility to make customers' experience as comfortable as possible.

Technology: It is true that every business nowadays needs appropriate technologies to function properly and fast. What are the most important technologies that your business requires? How will you procure and service them? You should provide a list of the key technologies your business cannot function without. Are the technologies proprietary or are made by a third-party? How do you plan to mitigate risks while using these technologies? Do you have any data security processes that you are going to employ in your business? Are you going to set up a helpful backup or recovery process if your business surprisingly comes under a cybersecurity attack?

Under this category, it is helpful if you can mention any proprietary technologies that your business already has. The proprietary technologies are the systems, tools, or processes that are unique only to your business and were internally built or developed for it. Investors are likely going to consider your business to be quite competitive if it has its own proprietary technology. This makes it difficult for competitors to beat you in your chosen industry.

Key customers: You should also include in your business plan your key customers. Will they be responsible for increasing your sales volume or for creating a new market for your products/services? In this section, you should identify all those customers that bring more than 10% of your overall sales. You should also indicate how you plan to keep them satisfied with your products. If you are just starting a business, it may be hard to actually determine who your key customers are. However, you can undertake some initial research to find who they are. These three approaches will be of invaluable help to your business:

- **Identify who the key customers of your main competitors are:** Pay attention to your main rival's customers. There is every possibility that the same caliber of customers will come to patronize your business. You can send someone to study your main competitors' stores or offices and ask questions about their key customers.

- **Test the waters:** You may need to send out questionnaires, interview prospective customers, and hand out free samples of your products for future customers to test. This may take time and cost you some marketing budget, but it is worthwhile if it is done properly.
- **Seek referrals:** People who are close to you may have an idea of customers that may like your products/services. So, ask them for referrals. Let them tell their friends, colleagues, neighbors, and partners. These referrals could end up becoming your key customers in the near future.

Key employees and their positions: In your business plan, you are required to provide a current organizational chart which will reveal the key personnel within the organization and the positions they hold, with their terms of service. You should describe their unique skills and qualifications that indicate how experienced they are to handle the tasks in your business. It may also be helpful to describe any proprietary recruiting and training practices in your organization. If you have an existing compensation plan, you may want to highlight some of its benefits here.

Note that potential investors will surely check out the list of your key employees: They would like to know if your team is capable of running the business well. The quality and levels of experience of your employees or partners can largely contribute to the overall performance of your business. So, you need to typically highlight the useful skills that your team possesses and make references to their past performances. For instance, you may want to describe your employee in this manner: "Mary James, B.A., M.A., has a five-years of experience working in sales. Her efforts have helped Newsbark Co. Ltd., her former employer, increase sales from $5 million to $15 million a year." As a matter of fact, detailed but concise information like this can sweep future investors off their feet.

Location or facility: As part of your business's operation plan, it is important to provide some information about your facility. Are you running a manufacturing plant, or will you only be working out of a rented office space? What are the necessary equipment or machinery in place to achieve uninterrupted business operations? Does your business outrightly own the facility or it is renting it from a third party? Does your business license permit you to run a business at such a location? What are the necessary legalities you have fulfilled to be able to run your business there? For example, if you don't have a permit to operate a restaurant, you may not be able to open your doors to customers without a well-designed and already inspected commercial kitchen.

Nowadays, it is not uncommon to find some business plans that contain facilities' floor plans. To be honest, this is a laudable and creative effort. A good facility floor plan will reveal distinct details about the facility that your proposed business will be using. It will show its space, the passages and, of course, the location of your equipment and machinery (if any). A floor plan is also useful if you are building your own factory from scratch. You will be able to see where each component of your business process will be situated. It is possible to make any necessary corrections from the floor plan before the entire factory or manufacturing plant is erected. This will save you a lot of money that would have been wasted on constructing a factory that may not be useful for your business in the long run.

You may not need to bother about a floor plan is you are renting your facility. However, it doesn't do any harm to just sketch it for your prospective investors to appraise. It will add value to your proposition and your reputation as a reliable and well-planned businessperson.

Another important piece of information about facility: it is advisable to have a facility that allows a long-time renting or lease. You don't want to keep changing your location every passing year. This is not only impractical and unsustainable, but it will also send the wrong signal to your partners and customers. You are required to indicate in your business plan the length of lease terms for your facility. That will give investors the peace of mind that you have a long-term goal to keep running your business from the same location.

Discussion Questions

1. Describe four important elements of an effective marketing plan.

2. Give two reasons why it is essential to have an operational plan provided in a business plan.

3. Can an organization function properly without a marketing and operational plan? Discuss.

Quiz

1. **You can't run a successful business without these two plans. What are they?**
   a. Information processing and data recovery plans
   b. Marketing and operational plans
   c. Compensation and pension plans

2. **Which of these is the costliest promotional option?**
   a. Word-of-mouth
   b. Friendly referrals
   c. Media buying

3. **Which of these is an important element in a marketing plan?**
   a. Organizational chart
   b. Payment
   c. Key message

4. **All of these pieces of information are required in an operational plan except:**
   a. List of technologies
   b. Organizational chart
   c. Promotional option

5. **What kind of information should be revealed in your organization chart?**
    a. Name of the key employees
    b. The positions of the key employees
    c. The salaries of the key employees

6. **What are proprietary technologies?**
    a. Technologies that your business has patents on
    b. Technologies belonging to a third party
    c. Technologies that you borrow from a partner

7. **Which of the following is not an example of traditional media?**
    a. Social media
    b. Newspaper
    c. Radio

8. **The process of delivering products/services to your customers through a well-planned supply chain is called.....**
    a. bookkeeping
    b. order fulfillment
    c. taxation

9. Providing your business's payment methods to prospective customers is a part of your business'.

a. operational plan

b. marketing plan

c. recruitment plan

10. Can you operate a restaurant business at a facility that has no commercial kitchen?

a. Yes, you can

b. No, you can't

c. I don't know

Answers	1 – b	2 – c	3 – c	4 – c	5 – c
	6 – a	7 – a	8 – b	9 – a	10 – b

Chapter Summary

- Your business's marketing plan is the blueprint for increasing sales and revenues by getting your key message out to prospective customers through well-planned promotional or advertising activities.
- Some of the great attributes of a well-designed operational plan is that it highlights all the necessary steps required for smoothly managing your business, from its inception to its growth and profitability.
  To estimate any business's average cost of sales or cost of goods sold, efforts must be deployed towards measuring the applicable metrics such as its inventory, cost of manufacturing, direct labor cost, and raw material expenses.

References

- Gallegos, J. (2019). Business plan 101. A guide to combine technical, financial, operational and marketing data that will not only get you funded but will actually help you operate your business successfully. Seattle: Amazon.

- Levinson, Conrad J, and Levinson, J. (2008). Startup guide to guerrilla marketing: A simple battle plan for first-time marketers. California: Entrepreneur Press.

Chapter 4

Doing Your Marketing Analysis

Starting a business is one thing, but finding the right markets (or customers) for your products and services is an entirely different aspect. Your business stands a high chance of surviving in the marketplace if you know exactly which market you are aiming to serve. In this section, you will discover some important elements of a well-prepared market analysis, how to use it, and what your business can gain from adopting it. A business plan without a detailed marketing analysis is incomplete. This is why you should pay serious attention to this chapter and carefully learn the essential steps required for designing an effective marketing analysis.

Key learning objectives should include the readers' understanding of the following:

- Do You Understand Your Industry?

- Which Market Segment Will You Be Serving? (describing their demographics)
- Who Are Your Major Competitors?
- SWOT Analysis
- What Are Your Business's Competitive Advantages?

4.1 Do You Understand Your Industry?

The business you are writing a business plan for belongs to a specific industry. It could be the financial, educational, healthcare, engineering, retail, legal, banking, or IT industry. A very important question is - How much do you know about your proposed industry? Dabbling into an industry you know nothing about is like wandering around a new city without a map or a guide. You don't want to waste your time and money setting up a business in an industry that may be difficult for you to succeed as a business owner.

Every shrewd entrepreneur equips themselves with the appropriate knowledge of the industry they are going to operate in. A typical industry analysis consists of the following pieces of information:

- **Industry participants:** These are the businesses and/or people that are already operating in the industry you want to enter. For instance, when you are talking about the Electric Vehicle (EV) industry, you will be counting Tesla, Google, Apple, and other EV companies as the current participants. It is very important to pay attention to the existing industry participants so that you can study, investigate, and plan to outsmart them in the industry. They are your competitors and you must analyze your business's strengths to compete with them. If you are going to set up a fast-food restaurant, the existing industry participants are McDonald's and KFC. You must enter into the industry with some special attributes that will help your business thrive among these established competitors. If you do not precisely know who your industry participants are, especially those who might pose a strong competition against your business, you may have to consider hiring a business development consultant to assist you with that. They will do the hard job of investigating, reporting, and analyzing your most formidable rivals in the industry. This will give you some knowledge of how to play safely in the market while still fending off these competitors. Every industry you can ever imagine is already crowded, but what will make a significant difference for your business is learning about the existing industry leaders and designing better approaches to solving the same problems that they are currently solving. It is your unique proposition that will make you thrive in an overcrowded marketplace. So, it is not technically sensible to enter into a market or an industry that you have little or no prior knowledge of. You should position your business for success right from the first day of operation.

- **Distribution patterns:** It is helpful to have a deep understanding of the distribution patterns in your chosen industry. How do the industry participants distribute their products/services? What supply chains are used in the industry? And how effective are the existing distribution patterns? Do you need to introduce a new system of delivery that is compatible with your business and is cost-effective as well? For example, if in an industry, the most preferable method of distribution is through retail stores and third-party distributorship, it may be unusual to sell your products through direct sales or business-to-business (B2B) channels. If you attempt to do that, you may surprise your prospective customers who were already used to the retailing approach, and you may end up spending a lot of money to advertise your products to spark enough B2B selling sales volume.

- **Competition and buying pattern:** You also need to study the competitive practices in the industry and investigate why customers will choose your rival over your business when making buying decisions. The survival of your business largely depends on its customer's willingness to continue buying from you. You can learn a lot from your competitors' customers and use the findings of your investigation to refine your sales strategies in order to win more buyers for your products.

- **Focusing on your main competitor:** Concentrate mainly on one competitor that may threaten the survival of your business. You need to critically analyze the following information about this main competitor: **Its product, pricing, reputation in the market, management structure, financial position, systems of product distribution, business development approaches, and brand awareness.** Knowing the most important data or facts about your main rival can equip you with the right amount of information to strategize how to outperform your competitor in the industry. In the corporate world, competitors do anything at their disposal to drive away customers from their rivals and kill their businesses. You must be ready at all times to compete effectively in the industry so as to save your business from a sudden collapse. The idea of focusing on your main competitors should be seen as a way to learn one or two good and positive things from them that you can use to transform your own business. You shouldn't see them as your "enemies". That negative perspective will obscure your judgment and possibly derail you from concentrating on how to engage in free and fair competition. In every country, running a business is considered a non-monopolistic endeavor. However, some companies, owing to their financial strength and quality of products/services can consequently outperform other businesses in their industry. This is natural, and the only effective way to be part of the leaders in your industry is to learn what others are doing and take those innovations to an entirely new and different level.

4.2 Which Market Segment Will You Be Serving (describing their demographics, geographics, buying habits, psychographics)

Every market is segmented in one way or the other. In other words, a market can be divided into different categories based on the demographics geographics, buying habits, and psychographics of the customers buying from it. For example, a shoe market can be divided into 4 or 5 segments or categories: We can have women's shoes, children's shoes, men's shoes, factory workers' shoes, and school kids' shoes. The same product (shoe) has different kinds of customers buying it for different purposes, in different parts of the world and in different age groups. So, whatever product you are making or producing, you need to fully understand the market segment you will be supplying your product to. Are they men or women, or both? What age groups do they belong to? Are they highly educated or moderately educated customers? What are their preferences when it comes to pricing, product types, and usefulness? Where do they live? Which ethnic, religious, or cultural groups do they belong to? What activities are they involved in?

If your market segment is from an older age group, take into consideration their needs and wants and how that affects their buying habits and mentality pertaining to your product or services.

The market segment you plan to serve may be extremely saturated and you need to know what you can do to differentiate your product or service. What makes your product or service different than all the other similar products or services in the market or the industry? For example, what makes your insurance agency different from other insurance agencies?

Your market segment may be phasing into a new market with a new set of customer characteristics, and it will definitely affect the way you market your product or service, and even the way the product is packaged and presented.

Take into consideration where in the world the product or service may be marketed. There are cultural differences and expectations accordingly that must be considered as you develop your product or service.

Therefore, in-depth market research is paramount to starting a business that will succeed and not fail. It is through this research you know what you need to do in order for your business to be successful.

You should provide adequate information about your proposed market segment in your business plan. Investors are always happy to invest in a business that already has a well-defined market segment it will be serving, because they know that some customers in your chosen market segment will be waiting to buy from your business.

Figure 4.1

Source : Shutterstock_402677080

4.3 Who Are Your Major Competitors?

You have read about how important it is to mostly focus on your main or major competitor in the industry you have chosen. Your business won't be operating alone in that industry: you will be competing for customers, market share, recognition, and growth rate with the other businesses or companies that are already in operation. You may need to highlight how you may outsmart this competitor in your business plan. Some of the information your investors may be interested in includes, but is not limited to:

- How will your business outperform your main competitor? What new systems or processes will you be implementing in your business operations that will transform the way you do business?

- Are your products/services unique and of high quality? Here is the hardest truth: you have no chance to ever outperform your rivals if your products/services are of lower quality or usefulness than theirs! Customers go to the sellers who offer the best things in town. It doesn't matter how much you are spending on marketing or advertising; you are not going to get anywhere if your products/services don't measure up to your competitors.

- Will your customers be willing and ready to spend their hard-earned money on your products/services? Yes, of course, if they like what they are served. However, they are likely going to shun your products/services if they don't help them solve their problems.

- What is your pricing system, and how can it differentiate your offerings from your competitors? Only a few business owners understand the power of pricing. No one is advocating that you should always price lower than your competitors. In certain circumstances, you may have to use competitive pricing techniques to keep your existing customers while reaching out to new ones.

- Do you have patents or proprietary trademarks that cannot be copied by other businesses? A company's long-time value depends on a number of factors. And one of them is the number of patents or proprietary technologies the business owns, which make it difficult for rivals to easily outdo the company in the industry.
- What is your product's shelf life? That is, how long can it stay on the shelf and become useful for your customers? No one wants to patronize a business that has products that are perishable in a short period of time. Customers constantly seek corresponding value for the money they spend.

Your answers to the questions above, carefully stated in your business plan, will demonstrate how formidable and strong your business is to withstand whatever competition comes its way.

4.4 SWOT Analysis

It is imperative that your business plan has a SWOT Analysis. The acronym SWOT stands for Strengths, Weaknesses, Opportunities, and Threats.

Figure 4.2 A SWOT Analysis Model

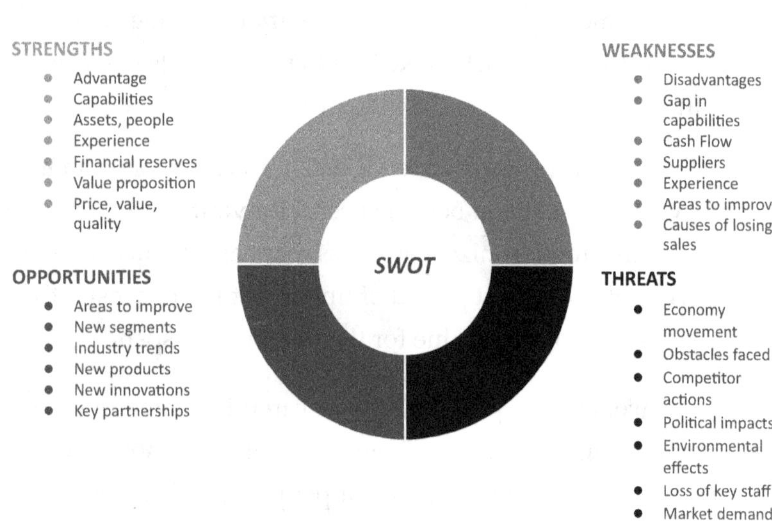

Source: A SWOT Analysis Model obtained from the Microsoft's Business Plan Template.

As shown in Fig. 4.2, you need to present some internal strengths and weaknesses of your business in your business plan. Similarly, your prospective investors will also be interested to know your business's external opportunities and threats that may affect its operations both in the long-term and short-term.

You can see in Fig. 4.2 the kinds of information/data/facts that should be presented in your SWOT Analysis. The model above provides all the necessary answers that your future partners and/

or investors will be looking for in your business plan. Without a well-presented SWOT Analysis, your business plan won't reveal so much information about what could affect your business' growth as it opens for day-to-day operations.

When designing your SWOT Analysis, pay attention to the following mistakes business owners often make when presenting their SWOT Analysis outcomes:

- **Long listing:** You are not expected to produce a long list for each of the four aspects of your SWOT Analysis. Make the list as short as possible. Avoid being repetitive; in fact, you should only list the main factors or points that mostly contribute to each SWOT Analysis section.
- **Overestimating strength:** Many new business owners err on this part—they volubly overestimate their strength to impress their business partners or prospective investors. This is not the right thing to do because you are exposing your business to failure right from the beginning. A business is like a machine; if you overstate its usefulness and overwhelm it with the functions it can do and cannot do, it will soon break down. Over expectations from customers, partners, and investors will drive you into exhaustion as you fight hard to impress others rather than genuinely running your business at its own pace.
- **Overlooking your weaknesses:** Not paying adequate attention to your business' weaknesses is as inappropriate and unhelpful as overstating its strength. One doesn't need a magical crystal ball to see that a business that promises to offer a product/service it doesn't produce is going to fail soon. Why? One of the errors of entrepreneur is to make flowery promises to customers but fall short in fulfilling

those promises. Such a business is not only going to lose some existing customers, but will also find it difficult to find new customers because it doesn't have a good reputation in the marketplace.

4.5 What Are Your Business's Competitive Advantages?

To survive in the intense competition that prevails in the marketplace, your business must demonstrate some competitive advantages over the others in the same industry. This majorly depends on which products/services you offer; however, your business stands a good chance of thriving if it has the following competitive advantages as well:

- **Better profit margin:** If it is cheaper for your business to make the same products that other companies produce expensively, you will have a better profit margin than your competitors. In this case, you will have a good cash flow that will streamline the process of running your business. Depending on the segments of customers you are serving, you can adopt different pricing systems or options. You could have a "freemium" option that allows customers to utilize your products/services for free for some time. You can also implement low-cost and premium pricing options. Your plan, as a shrewd business owner, is to make sure no one is left behind and that every customer has the opportunity to access your products/services, although they might do so in different stages of usage. You can build your profits into each pricing option as well, so that your business can have enough funds to run its business operations.

- **Proprietary products/services:** If you are bringing entirely new or innovative products/services to the marketplace, this can be considered to be one of your business's competitive advantages.
- **Good pricing:** Since it may not necessarily cost your business a lot to produce its great products, you can offer your customers good, competitive prices that may, in the long run, increase your sales volume.
- **Improved usefulness:** If your products are more useful than that of your competitors, your business has a significant business advantage over its rivals. It is common for customers to go for products or services that can serve their pressing long-term needs than those that are temporarily useful. This boils down to making great products that your customers can be proud of and eventually introduce to their friends. This is the logic behind the mad rush for luxury products. In spite of the fact that they are usually expensive, they offer better quality and can be used for longer timeframes. In the end, consumers believe that it was a sensible investment to put their hard-earned money into luxury goods because of their durability.
- **Better compatibility:** If your business is making electronics/electrical products such as hardware, software, and electronic products that are compatible with other related products in the marketplace, this may cause customers to choose your products over the others in the market. In addition to producing compatible products, you should also make sure that using your products alongside others won't affect their overall quality. This concern may be sorted out

with some other companies in your niche/industry whose products could be integrated with yours. For instance, before companies like Apple and Microsoft brings a new product to the market, they study how it could be easily integrated with other known products in the marketplace. More so, they would have agreed on some sharing formula of any proceeds when consumers use their software together to achieve a purpose.

You are expected to provide all these competitive and business advantages in your business plan so that when investors or prospective partners are going through the plan, they can quickly come to a conclusion about investing in your business.

Discussion Questions

1. What kind of information should your industry analysis reveal to anyone reading your business plan?

2. What are the four elements of a good SWOT Analysis, and why are they important?

3. Describe four ways how you can show that your business has some competitive advantages over your competitors.

Quiz

1. **What does T in the SWOT Analysis stand for?**
    a. Training
    b. Time
    c. Threats

2. **Which of these is the best way your business can differentiate itself from the others in the same industry?**
    a. Having proprietary products
    b. Running TV advertising
    c. Looking for an investor

3. **A market may be segmented into different categories because of all but one of these factors.**
    a. Age group
    b. Gender
    c. Accent

4. **When talking of industry participants, which of these companies will NOT be regarded as industry participants in the music industry?**
    a. Sony records
    b. Def Jam Recordings
    c. Tesla

5. One of the following is a weakness that a business may have.

a. Lack of cash flow

b. Qualified employees

c. Innovative products

6. One of the threats a business may confront while operating is

a. unexpected political impact

b. good employees

c. high profitability

7. Why should a business focus on its main competitor?

a. To learn how it is run and work to outperform it

b. To buy some products from it

c. To borrow funds from it

8. You have a great profit margin when……

a. It costs you $5 to make a product you sold for $6

b. It costs you $1 to make a product you sold for $6

c. It costs you $10 to make a product you sold for $6

9. Which of the following must be included in your business plan?

a. Marketing plan

b. Vacation plan

c. Employees' taxes

10. An investor will likely be willing to invest in your business if it has....

a. a good profit margin

b. a beautiful office

c. a long history of staying in business

Answers	1 – c	2 – a	3 – c	4 – c	5 – a
	6 – a	7 – a	8 – b	9 – a	10 – a

Chapter Summary

- You need to fully understand the industry your business will be operating in so as to win against your competitors in the same industry.
- Your business's competitive advantages are what differentiates it from others in the same industry.
- Use the SWOT Analysis model to show your business's Strengths, Weaknesses, Opportunities, and Threats before it starts operating.
- Focus your energy on your main competitors and learn how they run their operations so that you could know how to efficiently compete with them.

References

- Porter, Michael E. (1998). Competitive strategies: Techniques for analyzing industries and competitors. Washington, DC: Free Press.
- Stevens, Robert E., Loudon David L, Sherwood Philip K, and Dunn John Paul (2006). Market opportunity analysis: Text and Cases. New York: Routledge.

Chapter 5

Writing and Editing Your Business Plan

Now is the time to put together everything you have been researching and drafting about your business and its proposed operations! Are you excited about this last, major step? Well, you shouldn't feel overwhelmed in any way even if it looks like a cumbersome exercise. You should be aware of and avoid some common mistakes people often make when they are preparing their business plans. Take a deep breath as you carefully combine all the bits and pieces about your business on paper to be presented to your future investors as a useful business plan.

Key learning objectives should include the readers' understanding of the following:

- How to Organize Your Business Plan
- Common Mistakes People Often Make When Developing Their Business Plans

- Editing and Designing Your Business Plan
- Using a Business Consultant

5.1 How to Organize Your Business Plan

Every business plan consists of eight main elements. These elements could be perceived as the titles for each section of the plan which, in turn, have related subtopics.

Hence, these main elements of a business plan include:

1. **Executive Summary:** For your business plan's executive summary, you should write a page or a half-page description of your business using the suggested ideas below:

    - **Opportunities:** The problem that your business hopes to solve is the opportunity created in the marketplace. If you are an educational company, what aspect of schooling is your business addressing? Is it creating some learning tools or software for students? How are the products designed to achieve the highest rate of return (RoR) for you and your customer?
    - **Mission:** Your mission is your "why". Why are you starting or running a business?
    - **Solution:** What product/service are you offering to help your customers solve their main problem(s)?cc **Market focus:** What is the ideal market or the key customers you are targeting?

- **Competitive advantage**: What qualities separate your business from others?
- **Ownership:** Are you the sole owner of your business or you are in a partnership with other entrepreneurs or investors?
- **Expected returns:** What are your projected milestones for revenue, profits, growth, and customer maintenance?

NOTE: The Executive Summary should be written last, and it is essentially the "summary" of the main cogent points raised in the business plan. All the above-mentioned points can be woven into 2-3 short paragraphs on a single page.

2. **Company Overview:** The Company Overview should contain the following important information about your business. It is advisable that you should specifically address the most relevant information as briefly as possible because you will still have the chance to expand on them later under different sections. The rule of thumb is that your company or organizational overview should not be more than 1 or 2 pages.

    - **Company summary:** This should be considered as your "elevator pitch" in which you can quickly summarize what your business stands for and the short-term goals it hopes to achieve.
    - **Mission statement:** This is your business's guiding principle(s); it must clearly state all your primary goals for your employees, customers, partners, and the public.
    - **Company history (if any):** If your existing business has a history, don't hesitate to share it briefly.

- **Markets and services:** What are your target markets and what product/service is your business offering to fulfill the desire of the target customers in that market?
- **Operational structure:** You need to describe the employees on your business's payroll and the nature of their engagement. Are they qualified for their jobs?
- **Financial goals:** It is also expedient to present your business' financial goals. This is important information for your partners, suppliers, and investors to know.

3. **Business Description:** In this section, you will be required to provide detailed information about your business:

   - **Opportunity:** A business is mostly established to fill a need or fix a problem. In the course of doing this, opportunities are created and money is made. For example, Tesla was not initially created to make its founder rich, but it was founded to produce electric cars that would protect the environment from the destructive effects of fossil fuels.
   - **Product/service overview (what kinds of products/services are you offering to customers? And why?):** It is important to highlight the features or usefulness that will make your product/service unique and stand out from other products in the marketplace.
   - **Key participants:** It is advisable that you should outline some key participants who will be instrumental in the smooth running of your "business activities". They may be your suppliers, partners, distributors, or even your employees.
   - **Pricing:** This is where you are going to provide detailed information about your pricing options.

4. **Market Analysis:** The information that should be included in the marketing analysis includes:

    - **Industry type (use statistics):** Which industry will you be operating in? How much do you know about the internal workings of this industry?
    - **Market segmentation (use statistics):** Use statistics to present believable facts about the categories of customers that your business will be serving.
    - **Competition:** It is also imperative to provide some information about your competitors. If you have deep knowledge of the extent of competition that your business will be up against, that will equip you with the right amount of skills to thrive in the industry.
    - **SWOT Analysis**: This acronym stands for Strengths, Weaknesses, Opportunities, and Threats. You need to conduct a SWOT Analysis on your business and cleverly present it in your business plan.

5. **Operation Plan:** The operation plan should contain detailed information about your business's:

    - **Order fulfillment process:** You will need to explain the procedures your business will use to deliver products/ services to customers.
    - **Payment (which payment types are accepted?):** This must be stated clearly in your business plan. Sometimes when businesses offer a wide range of payment options, the number of customers increases.
    - **Technology (what are the necessary technologies your business will be using?):** Do you have some proprietary

technologies or tools? Mention all of them! If you are purchasing machines from other manufacturers, you may want to indicate which one in the plan.

- **Key customers (who are your customers? What demographics are they from? Their education, age group, etc.?):** Feel free to provide as many details as necessary about your key customers. Investors, as well as prospective partners, will be happy to lay their hands on such important information.
- **Key employees and organization (who will be managing the business?):** Outline your key employees' qualifications and experiences in your business plan. If they possess some enviable skills, don't hesitate to list those skills as well.
- **Facilities (what are the physical assets/facilities the business needs to operate?):** Describe your business' facility and explain why it is the best location for your business.

6. **Marketing and Sales Plan:** This section should provide all the necessary details about:

   - **Key messages/stories for your customers**: People like great stories; what motivates customers to fall in love with your products/services are the convincing stories they are told about how your product/service can solve their problems.
   - **Marketing activities—how to market your business's products/services, such as:**

     Media advertising (radio, television, newspaper, or magazine)

     Direct mail

     Telephone

Seminars or business conferences

Advertising partnerships with other businesses

Fixed signage

Word-of-mouth

Digital marketing like social media marketing, content marketing, SEO, or email marketing

- **Sales strategy (provide a list of your sales strategies):** It is important to describe in detail how your business will execute its sales strategy. Will you be using commissioned salespersons or hiring full-time sales professionals?

7. **Financial Plan:** Here, you can provide some information about your business's finances:

   - **Projected startup costs:** How much will it cost you to set up your business or how much will you be spending to keep running your existing business? Some new entrepreneurs sometimes run into problems while estimating how much their startup costs are. They either underestimate or overestimate costs.

   - **Source of funds for the business:** In your business's financial statements, it is a good practice to outline the sources of the funds for your business. You need to be transparent in every financial detail you are providing in the plan for investors and partners.

   - **Projected profit and loss model:** You should adopt a model to calculate your business's projected profit and loss.

   - **Financial documents/statements:** These are documents that will reveal the financial condition of your business. If you are taking investors' money, they will be interested in checking out your financial statements. If your business is new, you may have to produce financial documents that are based on future financial performance and projections.

- **Financial assumptions:** Businesses do make some assumptions while drafting their financial documents or statements. Those assumptions are internally decided upon. In other words, it may not be reasonable to utilize assumptions used by another business to support your own financial forecasting.

8. **Appendix:** This is where you put copies of all the documents, financial statements, or other essential papers that can provide support or additional details concerning your business activities.

5.2 Common Mistakes People Often Make When Developing Their Business Plans

New entrepreneurs or would-be business owners do make some mistakes when developing their business plans. Highlighted below are the six common mistakes people often make and how you can avoid them:

- **Not knowing their business well:** If you don't know your business well, you cannot clearly define the products/services your business will be offering to consumers and how it sets out to achieve that purpose. You need to be specific and bold when explaining what consumers stand to gain from using your products/services. Moreover, you should have profound knowledge about how to run your business and push it through growth and future expansion. As it is in life, so as it is in business. If you don't have a deep understanding of what you are doing, the chances are that you will be unable to convince anyone else to believe and support your cause. How would you react to a salesperson who knocked on your doors and whom you allowed into your living room, only for him to forget the facts about the products he was selling? Won't you immediately show him out the door? The same thing is applicable to you when you don't know your business pretty well. You will be confused and will mislead the people around you, i.e., your employees, partners, and investors.

- **Not having all the necessary details**: As indicated above, your business plan should have eight different sections. If you don't carry out your marketing analysis and draw up your business's financial projections, you will not be able to produce a conclusive business plan. Every section or element of the business matters, and each of them represents the necessary details that must be presented in your overall business plan.

- **Making unrealistic assumptions:** If you are yet to start your business, you may be tempted to make some unrealistic assumptions about the prospect of your yet-to-be-established business. For the purpose of swaying investors' decisions favorably towards your expectations, you may want to project unrealistic sales volumes or give bloated revenue figures. This won't help you in the long run. In fact, it could backfire if the investors discover that you are not being truthful. You may find it difficult to raise the funds you urgently need for your business. Always have this point at the back of your mind: deceptive assumptions won't take you very far. If you have succeeded in cajoling investors to part with their money and invest it in your business, they may soon discover your unrealistic exaggerations and call you to order. You may be lucky that they don't request for a refund of their cash or take legal action.

- **Not being flexible:** Here is a shocker: your business plan must be flexible enough to periodically reveal the concurrent changes that occur in your business operations. In other words, there is no definite approach for running a business; you may have to constantly update, rewrite, or revise your business plan in the light of drastic changes that may come your way while running your business. So, your business plan can never be so rigid that you refuse to embrace the transformations that happen during your entrepreneurship journey. Moreover, if you are running a partnership form of business, you will have to work cooperatively with your partners while making sensitive business decisions. This means that you will not always have your way when it comes to managing the business. In the same way, active investors do show tremendous interest in the day-to-day running of the businesses they have invested in. There will be instances where your investors or shareholders demand a certain course of action to be followed. It is important that you work flexibly with them because they may not always accept your opinions.

- **Dealing with analysis paralysis:** Every business owner experiences this condition once in a while. You may feel helpless and paralyzed and unable to act swiftly, due to over-analyzing the situation. The truth is that you cannot have all the answers from the beginning of your business—new methods or new techniques to run your business will always show up along the way. So, don't spend too much time searching for the perfect method of doing things, right from the onset. Be fast, methodical, and goal-oriented. Speed is something that is currently embraced in Silicon Valley, which is the American city in which most of the big tech companies in the world are headquartered. Why? If you want to become the industry leader, it shouldn't take forever to bring whatever innovative products you may be working on to the market. If you wait too long, other companies that may be working on the same product lines might bring theirs to the market before yours. This means that there will be more competition in the marketplace against your product.

- **Not seeking help when confused:** While preparing your business plan, you may run into some problems or difficulties. Rather than going ahead and developing an unrealistic business plan, it is advisable that you seek help from appropriate quarters. You may approach an experienced business owner or mentor to help you. Or you may even decide to contract a commercial business consultant to assist you in solving whatever problems that might have cropped up. You don't want to spend weeks or even months preparing a business plan that is of no practical use. You should never buy into the idea that a single person can make a great company or business. A successful business is built on the shoulders of some like-minded or goal-oriented individuals. Right from the onset, you may need to hire a business development consultant who will help you navigate many difficult issues that first-time entrepreneurs often face.

5.3 Editing and Designing Your Business Plan

After putting everything on the paper or typing it up in your word processor—all the necessary details about your proposed or current business—you will need to sit down to edit and design your business plan.

The checklist below will help you to do a great job of editing and designing your business plan:

- **Use a clean template:** If you are not a great document designer or not so good at using Microsoft Word (or some other word processing software), you may need to purchase a template online. In fact, there are some free templates for business plans online. Once you have chosen the best template that meets your appearance and color preferences, go ahead and transfer the content of your business plan onto it. Some people may choose to start developing their business plans using Microsoft Excel. Carefully transfer the content from Excel into your new template. If you don't know how to do this in a clean manner, you may decide to copy and paste the content into the new template.
- **Strictly follow the arrangement of the business plan's elements:** In order to sustain the flow and ensure that your business plan is easy to read, you should strictly present the content of your plan by following the eight elements of business already discussed in this book, starting from the Executive Summary and ending with the Appendix.
- **Pay attention to grammar and spelling errors:** Nothing spoils a business plan more than having grammar and spelling mistakes. If you are not good at proofreading or editing, you may want to ask someone who is better than

you to do that for you. Alternately, you may hire a freelance editor/proofreader to do that for you. The point is that your business plan should be rid of any grammatical or lexical errors that can make it difficult to digest by those who need to read it.

- **Fact-checking your numbers and details:** Spend some time fact-checking all the results of your analyses. Make sure your numbers are correct and the data in your business plan is factual. The essence of doing this is that you will be able to prepare a factual and detailed-oriented business plan that aligns with your integrity and professionalism. If you are citing data from other sources, confirm that they are genuine. It is a grave mistake to use incorrect data, assertions, and claims in your business plan. This can cause you more damage than you can imagine. A typical example of the danger of using unsubstantiated data is that it could mislead you into making decisions or assumptions that do not exist in the first place. Before you quote data or utilize statistics to support your arguments, make sure they are genuine. If you are not really sure about what is genuine or fake, you may need a fact-checker who will patiently go through the business plan to improve its clarity and authenticity.

5.4 Using a Business Consultant

A business consultant is someone whose primary responsibilities are to help business owners solve some of the problems that they may find difficult to handle by themselves.

These duties may include:

- Helping them draft, edit, and design their business plans
- Offering services that may include doing business analyses for them. Examples of these analyses are industry analysis, competition analysis, marketing analysis, sales planning, financial projections, operational planning, and so on.
- Providing consulting services that see a business owner through the entire business process, from starting his/her business to expanding its operations.
- As shown in the **Appendix,** a business consultant can also act as a business development consultant and offer accounting/bookkeeping services to business owners.

Discussion Questions

1. What are the four unique actions that must be taken to ensure that your business plan is properly edited and designed?

2. List the eight main elements of every effective business plan.

3. What are the six common mistakes people often make when developing their business plans?

Quiz

1. **There are ... main elements in every useful business plan.**
   a. 10
   b. 5
   c. 8

2. **Why is it important that you should always fact-check your business plan?**
   a. To change its color and appearance
   b. To make sure they are no lies or false claims in the plan
   c. To give your business plan a higher ranking on Google

3. **Which section of your business plan should put your company's "Mission Statement"?**
   a. Financial Analysis
   b. Company Overview
   c. Sales Analysis

4. **What is the ideal length for a business plan's Executive Summary?**
   a. 5 pages
   b. Half a page to one-page
   c. 25 pages

5. **What major benefit can a business owner derive from using the services of a business consultant?**

    a. To raise funding from the business consultant

    b. To receive much-needed assistance while developing their business plan

    c. To sell products/services to the business consultant

6. **When a business owner wastes much of his/her time analysis on every aspect of his/her business and is unable to make any concrete decision, it is referred to as....**

    a. SWOT Analysis

    b. Analysis paralysis

    c. Marketing Analysis

7. **One key part of your business's Operational Plan is....**

    a. media advertising

    b. order fulfillment process

    c. profit and loss model

8. **Which of the following piece of information should not be part of your Financial Plan?**

    a. The organizational chart

    b. Projected startup cost

    c. Profit and loss projection

9. Which section of your business plan includes the details about your current or proposed products and services?

a. Financial Plan

b. Business Overview

c. Executive Summary

10. A pragmatic business plan must also be....

a. flexible

b. inflexible

c. huge, with 200 pages

Answers	1 – c	2 – b	3 – b	4 – b	5 – b
	6 – b	7 – b	8 – a	9 – b	10 – a

Chapter Summary

- There are eight main elements of a functional business plan; if any of these elements is missing in your business plan, it may not as useful as you have expected it to be.
- To design a proper business plan, you must avoid the six common mistakes business owners often make.
- It is necessary to develop a business plan based on facts and truths, because if you included bogus claims in your plan, you may end up being rejected by investors.
- Grammatical errors and lexical mistakes (including typos) make it difficult for people to enjoy reading your business plan.
- If you are stuck while developing your business plan, you can consider hiring the services of a business consultant.

References

- Genadinik, Alex. (2015). How to write a business plan: Business planning made simple. Seattle: Amazon.

- Horan, Jim. (2019). The one page business plan professional consultant edition. Seattle: Amazon.

Chapter 6

Business Funding for Vet-Entrepreneurs

This chapter covers how U.S. military veterans may finance their startups. As a person who has served in the military, there are added perks for you in case you want to start a business. Included in this chapter are details regarding the grants, loans, and other means of raising the capital needed to cover the cost of starting a business. The purpose of this chapter is to act as a guide with information, resources, and sources that can be used to start a business with little or no out-of-pocket money outlay.

Key learning objectives should include the readers' understanding of the following:

- Know where to apply for business grants.
- Know where to apply for guaranteed business loans.
- Know how to capture and keep the attention of a potential investor.

- Be aware of Vet-Entrepreneur business resources.
- Know who to contact for one-on-one guidance and mentoring.

6.1 Applying for a business grant as a Vet-Entrepreneur

Military veterans have the discipline, leadership, and determination it takes to be successful business owners. Deciding to start one's own business takes courage and determination, not to mention the grit it takes to adapt and overcome challenging situations. Military members have a unique inroad to having the money to cover the cost of staffing, product development, service delivery, marketing, etc., as a perk for all the sacrifices in serving the United States. As a way of demonstrating honor to those who willingly went into battle frontlines, there are many special programs for vet entrepreneurs to obtain business grants for their businesses or startups.

Here is a partial list of the places where it is possible to obtain a business grant as a U.S. military veteran.

- ***Warrior Rising:***[2] For Veterans (serving or have served in the military), their widow(er), or their immediate family member, this 6-step application process must be followed:

Step 1-Automated application is completed in about 15 minutes.

2. *Warrior Rising.* Retrieved on June 19, 2022, from *Warrior Rising,* https://www.warriorrising.org/

Step 2-A phone chat takes place, and a decision to move forward with joining the Warrior Academy or work with a coach/mentor is made.

Step 3-Two times per month, there are virtual [group] 60-minute coaching sessions on the first and third Wednesday of the month.

Step 4-Entrepreneurs are invited to a Business Shower after a multi-step selection process, beginning with a coach, board/staff member, or mentor nomination. Apply and compete for a business grant.

Step 5-One-on-one mentoring takes place with the mutually agreed schedule between mentor and mentee for connectedness and accountability.

Step 6- Warrior Tribe is now your tribe, and you participate in Warrior Rising Events providing character development, fellowship, and networking.

Website for applying: www.warriorrising.org

- ***StreetShares Foundation***: For Active-duty military personnel (qualifying military member, spouse, child, or immediate family member), who owns at least 51% of the business, be at least 21 years old, this 4-step application process is required:

Step 1-View educational material by Street Shares.

Step 2-Application is made available.

Step 3-Write a summary of the business and submit a video.

Step 4-Up to 10 finalists are chosen and are presented to the public for a vote to determine the winners.

Website for applying: www.streetsharesfoundation.org/

- ***Grant Watch:*** For Veterans and service members. Most grants are for veterans helping veterans, for-profit and not-for-profit businesses. Website: https://www.grantwatch.com/cat/38/veterans-grants.html

- ***Veterans Small Business Grants:*** : For Veterans and active-duty military personnel, reservists, military spouses, and immediate family members. The grants are made possible by several methods, some not exclusive to veterans but just as helpful. Info site: www.veteran.com

- **Small Business Technology Transfer Program:** For American Veteran-owned businesses (with fewer than 500 employees) that carry out projects for the federal government. The grant is managed by the Small Business Administration (SBA), five other government agencies, and departments that accept business proposals, too. Up to two billion dollars are awarded to carry out the assigned projects. Up to two billion dollars are awarded to carry out the assigned tasks.

- **Small Business Innovation Research:** For American Veteran-Owned businesses (with fewer than 500 employees) to carry out designated innovation research projects. The SBA manages the grant, and 11 government agencies and departments participate in granting the money to carry out the research projects. Up to $850,000 is awarded to carry out the assigned task.See this video for more information: https://youtu.be/J1w8M3b7uVM

See this video for more information: https://youtu.be/J1w8M3b7uVM

Website for applying: www.sba.gov

Some business grants to veterans are available via associations and require paid membership for applicants to be considered. www.nase.org Become a member and get up to $4000 via the NASE Growth Grant. However, be aware that the annual fee is $99, the monthly payment is $11.99, and the benefits may or may not pay off in the end.

Also, be aware of the sites that charge money for their services when it is possible to research and see the information on your own, for free. An example of this is this site: www.usagrantapplications.org. The fee is $29.95. The price is refundable if not successful in obtaining a business grant. It may be a good investment since many applications are added to the site as per the types of grants that become available. Here is the place to apply: www.usagrantapplications.org

6.2 Applying for Vet-Entrepreneurship Business Loans

Business loans are abundant, especially for veterans with service-connected disabilities. The best and safest way to get a loan as a veteran-owned business is to contact the U.S. Small Business Administration. According to an article by Chloe Goodshore, "Business Loans, Grants, and Resources for Veteran Entrepreneurs," the SBA has a unique program for veterans with export businesses, as well as Express Loan and Military Reservice Economic Injury Disaster Loan programs that are SBA-backed loans.

Many lenders have APRs ranging from 2% to 22%. Compare the rates and see the best lender that makes the most sense using the website: www.business.org

6.3 Potential Investors for Vet-Entrepreneurs

Investors, especially Angel Investors, are seeking opportunities to show appreciation for those who had served in the military by underwriting their businesses or startups. However, some investors specialize in funding certain areas of industry such as a restaurant, retail store, pet boarding, childcare facility, veteran-owned businesses, etc. In most cases, it takes a little bit of time to know who these investors are and reach out to them.

Reaching out to investors takes courage and adequate preparations. Knowing how to communicate with them effectively is paramount to obtaining a positive outcome for veterans and investors. In most cases, the investor is putting more than money, which may include:

- Time
- Expertise
- Connections to customers or potential key members
- Connections to other investors
- Connections for other items for marketing, advertising, and publicity

Here is a list of some investors and venture capitalists that are focusing on businesses owned by veterans:

Hivers and Strivers (Early-Stage Investment): www.hiversandstrivers.com

Veteran Ventures Capital: www.veteranventures.us

Localvest: www.localvest.com

Academy Investor Network (must be a graduate from a military academy): www.academyinvestor.com

Meritorious: www.meritorious.us

Vet-Biz: (Must apply and be accepted for certification as a veteran business owner, women veteran business owner, disabled veteran business owner) www.vetbiz.va.gov

TFX Capital: For military members with professional and academic distinction and demonstrated ability to communicate, inspire and lead others while rallying a team to accomplish a mission. Must be able to learn, adapt, apply, and overcome unpredictable and always changing and challenging situations. Website: www.tfxcap.com

Context Ventures: This is a group of advisors with project management expertise seeking military members with leadership qualities to assist with the start and sustainability of the business. www.contextvc.com

Stony Lonesome Group: Partnering with post-911 Military Veteran entrepreneurs: www.stonylonesomegroupllc.com

Scout Ventures: For veterans with businesses in the technology industry such as AI, Data Science, Robotics, Drones, Autonomous

Mobility, AR/VR, Advanced Materials, Physical and Cybersecurity, Quantum Computing, Space, and Enterprise SaaS. www.scout.vc

Moonshots Capital: For veterans with world-changing companies. www.moonshotscapital.com

LunaCap Ventures: Provides debt-financing to military, women, and minority founders. www.lunacapventures.com

Folla Capital: Crowdfunds to help veterans raise the capital needed to start a business. www.follacapital.com

6.4 Franchising for Veterans

For veterans who want to have a business by owning a franchise, check out the resources provided below:

Franchise Direct - www.franchisedirect.com

VetFran - www.vetfran.org

6.5 Vet-Entrepreneurs Business Resources

As was mentioned in the previous chapter, there are many ways to obtain the required funding to start a business. Below are five business funding resources for veterans that might be a good fit for you.

- **Veteran Business Outreach Center (VBOC):** The U.S. Small Business Administration (SBA) has a special program for vet entrepreneurs to train, mentor, and assist them as they plan and operate the business during the period between leaving the military and living a civilian life. Mentoring and counseling among other programs are resources in this program.
- **Veteran Women Igniting the Spirit of Entrepreneurship (VWISE):** This program is one of several programs by the D'Aniello Institute for Veterans & Military Families for female vet-entrepreneurs. This program is designed to assist with the start and sustainability of a female veteran-owned business by providing training and mentoring in a community of highly successful women veteran and military spouse entrepreneurs. www.ivmf.syracuse.edu
- **Boots to Business (B2B):** The SBA has a special program designed to help military members plan, manage, and grow their businesses. This program is provided in the transition from military life to civilian living in the Department of Defense Transition Assistance Program (DOD TAP). Service members and their spouses are eligible to participate in this program. www.sba.gov
- **Veteran Readiness and Employment:** The Department of Veteran Affairs has a program for military members with

severe service-connected disabilities that includes issuing a business grant to start their own business. There is an application form to complete VA Form 28-1900, and then a chat with a VR&E counselor. www.va.gov

- **Veterans Entrepreneurship Program (VEP):** The Department of Veteran Affairs of the Small & Disadvantaged Business Utilization has a special portal by military veterans start or grow their own business. The program is designed specifically for military members with service-connected disabilities and veterans with distinguished leadership while serving in the military.
- **Vet to CEO:** Free program to transitioning warriors for a business accelerator program; nine weeks, virtual, one night per week, from 7-9 pm EST from August 30th to October 25th. www.vettoceo.org
- **SCORE Special program for Vet-Entrepreneurs:** Metaboost includes webinars" From Veteran to Entrepreneur – Steps to Start and Find Funding, Are You the Next Veteran Entrepreneur? Vet-to-Vet Advice About Business Ownership, and From Battle to Business: How the Military Prepared Me for the Corporate World. www.score.org
- **Bunker Labs:** Business entrepreneurship training, mentoring, and assistance with all aspects of running a business. This program has labs, classes, webinars, and networking sessions for vet entrepreneurs to gather together and share expertise. www.bunkerlabs.org

6.6 Contract-Awarding Programs

The US. government agencies have a program for accepting contracting bids from veteran business owners, and even more, this is a set-aside opportunity for disabled veteran business owners.

Veteran business owners need to register their businesses and be certified using the SAM registry: www.usfcr.com

Discussion Questions

1. If a veteran wants to own their own business but is unsure if they want to start it, take over a business already in operation, or purchase a franchise, where would they go to get advice?

2. Is it possible to get a business grant, a loan, and a business arrangement with an investor?

3. If you have a non-profit organization, is it possible to create a business loan?

4. Do you know where to go to ask questions, get technical assistance, get funded, or get a business mentor as a veteran business owner?

Quiz

1. **Which statement is true:**
   a. You must pay back the money from a business grant.
   b. You do not have to pay back guaranteed business loans.
   c. You must pay back a business loan, not a business grant.
   d. All these statements are false.

2. **Which of these sources can be used to fund a veteran business startup**
   a. Warrior Rising Business Grant
   b. Hivers and Strivers business grant
   c. VetFran
   d. All the above.

3. **A Vet-Entrepreneur seeking business advice goes to:**
   a. Family and friends
   b. SCORE
   c. VBOC
   d. Both b and c

4. **Warrior Rising helps with:**

    a. Franchising

    b. Lines of Credit

    c. Business grant and coaching

    d. None of the above.

5. **Investors want to invest in:**

    a. Time

    b. Expertise

    c. Connections

    d. All of the above.

6. **This company helps with investment funding:**

    a. Hivers and Strivers

    b. Warrior Rising

    c. VetFran

    d. VetBiz

7. ***StreetShares* Foundation assists with:**

    a. Franchising

    b. Investments

    c. Lines of Credit

    d. Business grants

8. All but one of these are veteran business sources.

a. Boots to Business

b. Franchise Direct

c. Vet to CEO

d. Veterans Entrepreneurship Program

9. Veteran Readiness and Employment is run by which agency:

a. Department of Labor

b. Department of Veteran Affairs

c. Boots to Business

d. Veteran Business Outreach Center

10. Which statement is true:

a. Bunker labs have training, mentoring, and assistance for running a business.

b. Veteran business owners do not need to register the business with the SAM registry.

c. Starting and finding funding for a veteran business owner is nearly impossible.

d. None of these statements are -true.

Answers	1 – c	2 – d	3 – d	4 – c	5 – d
	6 – a	7 – d	8 – b	9 – b	10 – a

Chapter Summary

- There are several places where a military member may obtain a business grant, loan, or investor.
- A business loan must be paid back, whereas a business grant is money that is not required to be paid back.
- Investors want to invest more than money; they want to invest time, expertise, technical assistance, and connections.
- Meeting the criteria for the business grant, loan, or investor is what is needed. After fulfilling all the requirements, the rest of the process begins.
- Having a service-connected disability rating of 10% or greater allows contracting with the government as a set-aside, allowing contract bids from veteran business owners to be readily accepted.
- It is prudent for the vet-entrepreneur to reach out and access the business resources available, especially to maneuver the business minefield to have a successful business journey

References

- 6 Small Business Grants for Veterans (And other funding resources). Retrieved from Forbes on June 19, 2022, https://www.forbes.com/advisor/business-loans/small-business-grants-for-veterans/

- 149 Grants for Veterans (n.d.) *Grant Watch.* Retrieved on June 19, 2022, https://www.grantwatch.com/cat/38/veterans-grants.html

- Apply for Veteran Readiness and Employment with VA Form 28-1900 (n.d.). *U.S. Department of Veteran Affairs.* Retrieved on June 19, 2022, https://www.va.gov/careers-employment/vocational-rehabilitation/apply-vre-form-28-1900/start

- Black, M., & Tarver, J. (2022, March 28) 6 Small Business Grants for Veterans (And Other Funding Resources). *Forbes Advisor.* Retrieved on June 19, 2022, https://www.forbes.com/advisor/business-loans/small-business-grants-for-veterans/

- Goodshore, C. (2021) Business Loans, Grants, and Resources for Veteran Entrepreneurs. *Business.org.* Retrieved on June 19, 2022, https://www.business.org/finance/loans/veteran-business-loans-and-grants/

- Military Benefits (n.d.) Small Business Grants for Veterans. *Veterans.com.* Retrieved on June 19, 2022, https://veteran.com/small-business-grants-veterans/

- Moores, E. (2021) Small Business Grants for Veterans. Fast Capital 360. Retrieved on June 19, 2022, https://www.fastcapital360.com/business-loans/guides/veteran-business-grants/

- SBA Business Loan Information for Veterans (n.d.) *U.S. Small Business Administration.* Retrieved on June 19, 2022, https://www.sba.gov/content/sba-business-loan-information-veterans-0
- Seppala, E. (2020) 5 Grants Your Veteran-Owned Small Business or Start-up Could Get in 2022. Merchant Maverick. Retrieved on June 19, 2022, https://www.merchantmaverick.com/business-grants-veterans/
- The Veteran Small Business Award (n.d.) *Street Shares Foundation.* Retrieved on June 19, 2022, https://streetsharesfoundation.org/the-veteran-small-business-award
- U.S. Small Business Administration (n.d.) Retrieved on June 19, 2022, https://www.sba.gov/about-sba-navigation-structure/technology-sbirsttr
- Veteran Business Grants. Retrieved on June 19, 2022, from Fast Capital360, https://www.fastcapital360.com/business-loans/guides/veteran-business-grants/
- Veteran Readiness and Employment (Chapter 31) (n.d.). *U.S. Department of Veteran Affairs.* Retrieved on June 19, 2022, https://www.va.gov/careers-employment/vocational-rehabilitation/
- Veterans Small Business Grants. Retrieved on June 19, 2022, from Small Business Grants for Veterans, https://veteran.com/small-business-grants-veterans/
- U.S. Small Business Administration Technology. Retrieved on June 19, 2022, from SBA, https://www.sba.gov/about-sba-navigation-structure/technology-sbirsttr

Glossary

1. **Disabled veteran** – a person who served or is serving in the military with a service-connected disability rating of 10% or greater.

2. **Set-asides**- The US government sets aside contract bidding as a certain percentage for veterans and veterans with a service-connected disability to bid and be accepted for contracted jobs and projects.

3. **Small business**- determined by the number of employees or revenue based on the company's industry. See the table: https://www.sba.gov/document/support-table-size-standards.

4. **Veteran**- a person over 18 years of age that served in the military past the basic training phase and is no longer actively involved.

5. **Vet-Entrepreneur**- a person who served in the military or currently serving in the military owning or plans to own a business with 51% or greater ownership.

6. **Warrior**- a person over 18 years of age, currently actively involved in serving in the military service with the Army, Air Force, Navy, Marines, Coast Guard, or Space Force in either a full-time or part-time capacity, drilling, deployed, or mobilized.

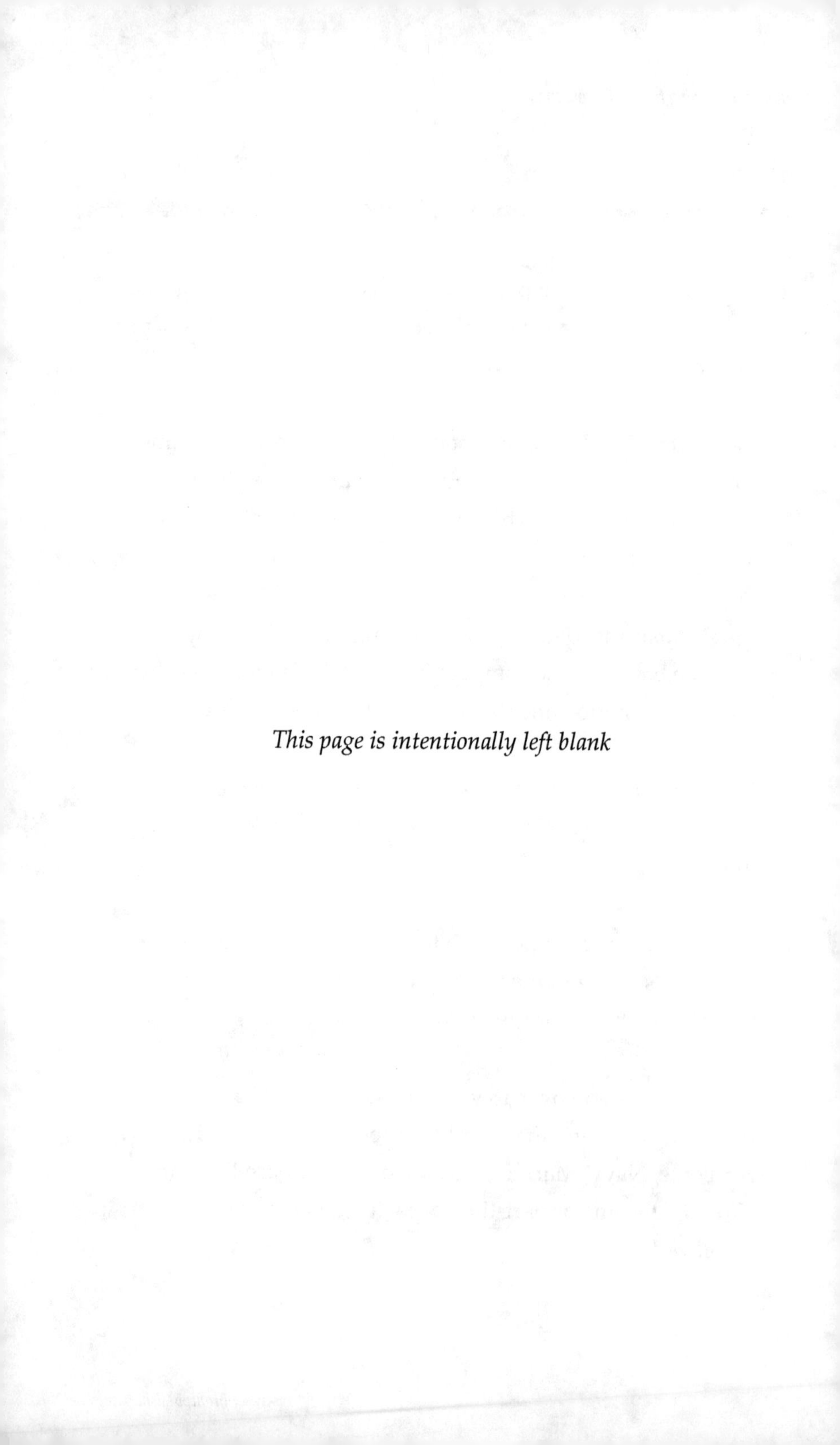

This page is intentionally left blank

Chapter 7

Business Plan for Nonprofits

You should always provide a specific business plan for a certain purpose. Why? The business plan that will be used for a nonprofit organization may not be useful for an engineering company that undertakes a manufacturing business. That's why it is important to produce a business plan that matches the nature of the business that you are venturing into.

Key learning objectives should include the readers' understanding of the following:

- All You Need to Know about Developing A Business Plan for Nonprofits
- A Sample Business Plan for Nonprofits

7.1 All You Need to Know about Developing a Business Plan for Nonprofits

A nonprofit business plan is different from every other business plan in the sense that it is designed to address an entirely different area of human endeavors. Outlined below are seven things you should consider while developing a nonprofit business plan:

- **Fundraising:** As its name implies, you are not expected to cash in on or make a profit from the activities of your nonprofit organization. So, that realization shuts your nonprofit out of the regular or traditional methods of raising money. Venture capitalists are only interested in making money and their business goals are not aligned with the principle behind running a nonprofit organization. Therefore, you are expected to provide the details of your fundraising process in this business plan.

- **A very strong mission statement:** A nonprofit mission statement must express, in strong terms, the critical mission that the nonprofit organization is trying to pursue. Examples are fighting drug addiction, prostitution, gang violence, or any other good cause. This mission statement must be worded in a manner that enables every reader of the business plan to see how each part of the plan holds up the central goals of the organization.

- **Well-defined demographics:** It is important that the population that the organization aims to serve must be clearly defined. Are they trafficked individuals, drug addicts, or prostitutes? Efforts must be made to ensure that there is uniformity in the content of the business plan.

- **What kind of services?** Nonprofit organizations are mostly service-based. Hence, it is imperative that their unique services must be outlined and explained in detail. These services must align with the organization's mission statement. The modes of service delivery must also be clearly stated.
- **Marketing approaches:** Due to their nature, nonprofit organizations are selective in their marketing drive. Most of them rely on word-of-mouth or outreaches organized by them. You can hardly find a nonprofit being advertised via digital media because they do not know or cannot control where their advertisements will be placed. They do not have the authority to order a digital marketer not to place their anti-drug addiction advertisement on a website that encourages careless lifestyle and drug abuse.
- **Organizational chart:** It is possible for a company to avoid placing its organizational chart in a business plan; however, every senior decision-making member of a nonprofit organization must appear in its organizational chart. This gives the public the opportunity to scrutinize them and be sure they are dealing with individuals with good credibility and character.
- **Ethics and standards:** It is advisable that you must conform to every ethical consideration or standard that guides the operations of the nonprofit organization you are preparing a business plan for. This is necessary because it will portray the organization as a legal and ethical entity that other nonprofits may be interested in partnering with.

7.2 A Sample Business Plan for Nonprofits

This sample is meant to demonstrate how a business plan for any nonprofit organization should be drafted. However, you are required to flesh out all the appropriate sections after gathering all the applicable data or information that would go into the business plan.

Title: A Business Plan for **Sunshine Forever**—A Nonprofit Organization that caters to people that have stopped abusing substances such as drugs, alcohol, and other stimulants.

Executive Summary

Sunshine Forever, a rehabilitation concept, will be located in New York City. The organization aims to provide an opportunity for people that are transitioning from their harmful behavior associated with substance abuse to reintegrate into society without any feeling of guilt or recrimination.

New York City has struggled under the influence of substance addiction for years. The statistics reveal that 3.7% of New York residents have reportedly used some illicit substances, causing about 9.2 per 100,000 people to lose their lives annually through drug-induced deaths.

Sunshine Forever will harness the power and willingness of its prospective volunteers, comprised of experienced health practitioners, social workers, and other professionals, to set up regular counseling sessions for addicts that are willing to transition into a drug-free lifestyle.

Sunshine Forever aspires to reduce the population of people that abuse substances in New York City by at least 0.1 % yearly for the next 10 years. Funds for this operation will be raised from the public, private organizations, and other well-wishers.

Organizational Overview

Mission Statement: Sunshine Forever believes that when people are given the care and attention that they crave, they will be able to listen, interact, and choose to live a better, drug-free life that will turn things around for them. The organization promotes the use of positive reinforcement and affirmations to improve the affected persons' thoughts and allows them to freely make the switch. In other words, no one will be threatened or coerced to embrace a new and healthier lifestyle; they should be able to reason within themselves, encouraged by professionals, to start living a life worthy of admiration and praise.

Sunshine Forever will liaise and collaborate with all Federal, state, and county apparatuses in making sure that all its operations are legitimate and within the ambit of laws and regulations that allow transformative therapies.

Service Description

Sunshine Forever will undertake rehabilitating procedures that may include but are not limited to any of the following:

- Locating where the most vulnerable drug addicts are residing

- Bringing them to the Sunshine Forever center, once they have agreed to talk (as opposed to forcing them to come to the Center)
- Providing initial hygiene for them, such as letting them take their baths, have some necessary medical examinations, and be well-fed
- Housing those who have agreed to go through the rehabilitation process at Sunshine Forever
- An average rehabilitation session is expected to last for 5-10 weeks, during which their progress will be closely monitored. If at any time any of the addicts refuse to cooperate with the professionals helping him/her, they will be allowed to depart from the premises

Market Analysis

The main demographics served by Sunshine Forever are drug addicts or individuals abusing substances that may put their lives at risk.

They could be of any age and gender, but special consideration will be given to women who have children with them. Sunshine Forever believes that such an action could produce a positive multiplier effect in the sense that if they are sober after being fully rehabilitated, they can save their children from going through the same ordeal.

Operating Plan

Organization Chart: Every volunteer that will work for Sunshine Forever will be vetted to make sure they are people of noble character and have got no criminal convictions that may undermine their integrity while volunteering for Sunshine Forever.

Facility: Sunshine Forever plans to run a rehabilitation center where addicts can come to receive their counseling sessions, that may last anywhere from 5 to 10 weeks. They will also be given a unique opportunity to live in some accommodations provided by Sunshine Forever. These could be houses, apartments, or dormitories under the administered Sunshine Forever.

Volunteers: Sunshine Forever looks forward to working with any professional from all walks of life. They could specialize in any field and could make themselves available for further training as and when needed. There are many things to do at the Sunshine Forever's facility, so everyone is welcome. However, there will be an emphasis on credible character and a great deal of professionalism will be required of every volunteer that chooses to work with the organization.

Marketing and Sales Plan

Sunshine Forever doesn't plan to buy any media advertising. It will be relying on word-of-mouth, signage, and participation in religious and cultural activities in the locality where it is established. The goal is to have at least one Sunshine Forever facility established in every state in the United States.

Financial Plan

To run its operations, Sunshine Forever will conduct a monthly fundraising, which is expected to be attended by invited philanthropists, private and state organizations, and religious and cultural organizations. The funds obtained will be properly documented and publicly uploaded to Sunshine Forever's website so that the public and other relevant authorities can be updated. Sunshine Forever will be transparent and law-abiding in all its activities.

Below is a projected income statement, statement of financial position, balance statement, and cash flow statement for the fiscal year ending December 31, 20XX.

Income Statement for the fiscal year ending December 31, 20XX

Revenue: $1 million

Total Expenses: $800,000

Net Income Before Taxes: $200,000

Statement of Financial Position as of December 31, 20XX

Cash and Cash Equivalents: $30,000

Receivables: $500,000

Property and Equipment: $2 million

Intangible Assets: $0

Total Assets: $2.53 million

Balance Statement

The board of directors has approved the 20XX fiscal year budget for Sunshine Forever, which is estimated at $1 million in revenues and $800,000 in expenditures. This reveals that the organization is profitable at the end of the fiscal year, even though making tangible profits is not the sole reason for running the organization.

Cash Flow Statement for the Fiscal Year Ending December 31, 20XX

Operating Activities: Income Before Taxes -$200,000

Investing Activities: New equipment and supplies -$50,000

Financing Activities: Fundraising campaign $600,000

Net Change in Cash: $350,000

According to the 20XX fiscal year financial statements for Sunshine Forever, it expects its investments to decrease by 2 percent and it is projected to generate $1.3 million in revenues. Its total assets are valued at $2.53 million, which comprises of equipment and property worth about $2 million dollars.

Appendix

This is where all other documents necessary for running Sunshine Forever will be placed.

Discussion Questions

1. Why is it important to clearly state a nonprofit organization's mission statement?

2. Give the main reason why a nonprofit organization may not choose to raise funds from a venture capitalist firm?

3. Why should everyone be aware who is on the organizational chart of a nonprofit organization?

Quiz

1. **Which of these is a visible part of a nonprofit organization's business plan?**
   a. Methods of fundraising
   b. Physical address of its office
   c. The marketing plan

2. **Can a nonprofit organization raise money from a venture capitalist?**
   a. No, it can't
   b. Yes, it can
   c. I don't know

3. **What kind of a nonprofit is Sunshine Forever?**
   a. It gives money to people that lack money
   b. It provides food for the homeless
   c. It rehabilitates people suffering from substance addiction

4. **In which City will Sunshine Forever be located?**
   a. California
   b. New Mexico
   c. New York

5. **How long does a rehabilitative session last for each of the addicts at Sunshine Forever's facility?**

   a. 1-5 weeks

   b. 5-10 weeks

   c. 30-50 weeks

6. **What is Sunshine Forever's projected net income before taxes?**

   a. $400,000

   b. $200,000

   c. $1.5 million

7. **What is projected value of the nonprofit organization's total asset?**

   a. $2.53 million

   b. $1.53 million

   c. $500,000

8. **What kinds of volunteers is Sunshine Forever looking to work with?**

   a. Any well-manner professionals

   b. Only medical doctors

   c. Only university students

9. Looking at the balance statement of the nonprofit organization, is it at a loss or does it make some profit at the end of the fiscal year?

a. It is profitable

b. It is losing money

c. I don't know

10. Which of these advertising methods will not be used by Sunshine Forever?

a. Word-of-mouth

b. Signage

c. Television

Answers	1 – a	2 – a	3 – c	4 – c	5 – b
	6 – b	7 – a	8 – a	9 – a	10 – c

Chapter Summary

- The business plan for a nonprofit organization differs from other business plans in the sense that it is not a profit-making organization. Hence, attention is mostly drawn to its mission state, methods of marketing, and fundraising.
- Efforts must also be deployed towards revealing, in detail, how a nonprofit organization attempts to remain ethical and standard-oriented while carrying out its statutory services.
- A nonprofit organization can utilize the services of volunteers, but their actions must be guided by the applicable Federal, State, and County laws and regulations.

References

- Anheier, Helmut, K. (2014). Nonprofit organizations: Theory, management, policy. New York: Routledge.

- Heyman, Darian, R. (2016). Nonprofit fundraising 101: A practical guide to easy-to-implement ideas and tips from industry experts. New Jersey: Wiles & Sons.

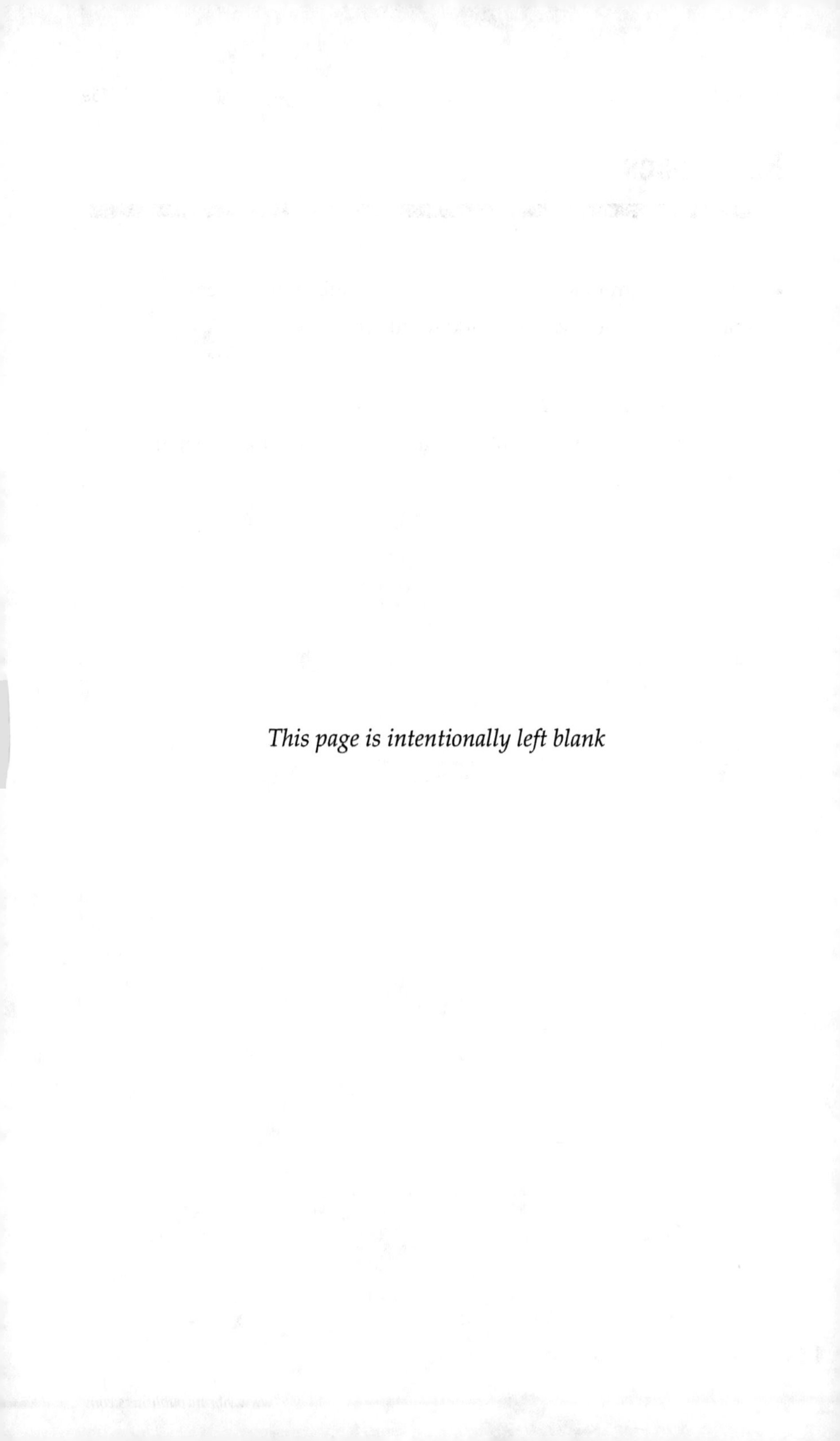
This page is intentionally left blank

Chapter 8

Business Plan for a Small Service Business

Preparing a business plan for a service business requires that you have deep knowledge of the service(s) you are offering to consumers. You could be an event planner, a lawyer, a mechanic, or even a business consultant. The common characteristic of all service businesses is that you are selling your time and service in return for some kind of payment. What mainly separates a service business plan from a product business plan is that there is a comparatively low cost of goods sold for the service businesses. In other words, you don't necessarily have to spend a lot of money to sell your services as opposed to selling your products. Moreover, service businesses have little or no inventory, which is a good thing.

Key learning objectives should include the readers' understanding of the following:

- Techniques for Developing A Great Business Plan for A Small Service Business
- A Sample Business Plan for A Small Service Business

8.1 Techniques for Developing A Great Business Plan for A Small Service Business

The best approaches for writing an effective business plan for a small business entails that you pay serious attention to the following criteria:

1. **Description of your service(s):** You must clearly and comprehensively describe the service or a line of services that your business will be carrying out. It should be detail-oriented and understandable enough for those that will read your business plan, be it an investor or a future partner. It is advisable that you highlight some of the distinguishing qualities that separate your services from the others in the same industry. In short, your value proposition (the value to be delivered through your service(s)) must be realistic and acceptable to consumers. You may also want to state your prices for the services, justifying why consumers should patronize your services with such a price tag.

2. **Creating a strong marketing plan:** You need to create a formidable marketing plan for your service business. Even if your services are great, people may still not discover them if

you don't advertise whatever you are offering. Your marketing plan should be genuine, practical, and doable. Generally, you can use both traditional and digital marketing processes to bring your services to the attention of your prospective customers. Whichever approach you take, you should make sure it is impactful and cost-effective. The best way to reach your future customers is to utilize the common means of marketing in your chosen industry. Investors, for the most part, are more interested in seeing how you plan to effectively win the hearts of future customers than spending time to appreciate the quality of your services.

3. **Do you know your numbers?** "Knowing your numbers" refers to fully understanding your financial position or condition. Starting a small service business requires money. How much is your expected startup costs? Where do you expect to get the funding from? How much revenue do you project that your services will bring in during the first, second, or third year of operation? Will your service business be profitable in the short- or long-term? What are the facilities, equipment, and tangible assets that will be required to kickstart your business operations? It is expedient to provide concrete answers to the above-mentioned questions in order to prove to investors or future partners that you have a fundamental knowledge of the business you are planning to start.

4. **Designing your operational plan:** What matters most in providing a service or a line of services is to satisfy your customers. To achieve this, it is imperative that your service delivery must be streamlined, fast, and efficient. You need a doable operational plan to smoothly run all your business processes. A typical operational blueprint will contain the necessary information or guidelines about the appropriate

strategies you will adopt for executing each step of your business operations. When navigating an unknown terrain or street, a directional map is of immense help. In the same way, a useful operational plan will take you from where you are to where you want to be as a responsible service provider.

8.2 A Sample Business Plan for A Small Service Business

You can use this sample business plan for a small service business to guide you in designing your own. The information provided here demonstrates how best to prepare your business plan as a service provider. So, you will be required to supply exact information about your own business in the plan.

Executive Summary

Sanders Infotech is a Software as a Service (SaaS) business that provides enterprise solutions for small- and mid-sized companies. Sanders offers a suite of Customer Relationship Management (CRM) software services to help enterprises maintain good relationships with their customers.

Based in Nashville, Tennessee, Sanders Infotech uses the latest SaaS technologies to help its customers design beautiful frontend systems. These systems facilitate the procedures of obtaining, processing, storing, and retrieving customers' data that Sanders Infotech's customers can use to make informed, company-wide customer service decisions.

Customers can subscribe to this service while utilizing Sanders' affordable cloud technology.

Company Overview

Sanders Infotech is a Limited Liability Company (LLC) that is founded by two people, Mr. King James and Ms. Diana George, who each own fifty percent of the company.

Sanders has been established to primarily help businesses manage their CRM systems. Good customer service is very essential for increasing revenue and achieving a high profitability rate. Unfortunately, not all companies have a great CRM process in place, and Sanders infotech has been created to help them bridge the gap in their CRM systems.

Business Description (Service Description)

Customers can subscribe to the three types of Customer Relationship Management services offered by Sanders Infotech, namely CRM 1, CRM2, and CRM 3. Monthly and annual subscriptions are possible.

CRM 1: This system is deployed to help companies obtain vital data from their customers. It also has in-built data processing, storing, and retrieval features. Businesses can measure the responsiveness of their customers to their customer service activities and see if certain desirable metrics are met.

CRM 2: This is a telephony/communication software that streamlines the communication and interaction between businesses and their many customers. This tool can be customized based on the company's size and requirements.

CRM 3: This is an accounting tool that tries to match CRM efficiency with revenue generation. There are some metrics in the software that helps businesses identify if a better customer service is leading to more sales, revenues, and, of course, higher profitability.

The entire CRM architecture is managed by experienced frontend and backend programmers and data scientists who will work closely with each business in customizing the much-needed CRM tools.

Customer Service Management software will always be in high demand as companies explore ways to increase sales and actualize their profitability expectations.

Market Analysis

Sanders infotech will target small- and medium-sized companies that aim to improve their customer service management procedures. The expected customers will be found in all industries, and their locations are immaterial. In other words, Sanders Infotech will be providing CRM services globally.

SWOT Analysis: The strength of Sanders Infotech lies in its capacity to serve businesses having different sizes. More importantly, the technologies developed by Sanders are proprietary and have been patented or trademarked.

One major weakness Sanders Infotech possesses is that it has to compete with other CRM companies that are already in the marketplace.

Sanders can explore the opportunities in emerging economies of third-world countries that have companies that seriously need its proprietary technologies.

The major threat against a wide application of Sanders Infotech CRM technologies is that it is currently in English. This means that it cannot be localized to other languages at the moment, but Sanders will work on achieving that in the next 5 years.

Operating Plan

It is expected that well-trained, in-house tech professionals comprising of experienced software and software engineers and data scientists will oversee the day-to-day operations of Sanders Infotech. More importantly, the professionals have had hands-on (practical) experiences in the Customer Service departments of other companies before joining Sanders Infotech.

Customers will be able to pay for the CRM solutions offered digitally and through bank transfers.

Sanders' business operations will be managed at its physical office located in Nashville, Tennessee, but there is a plan to also hire some outsourced professionals or resources when necessary.

CRM 1, CRM 2, and CRM 3 are cloud-based and customers can operate entirely in the cloud. They are not expected to own any hardware; they are only required to download Sanders Infotech's apps (both windows and mobile).

Marketing and Sales Plan

All marketing avenues will be explored to promote Sanders' CRM solutions, including both traditional and digital marketing channels.

The key message to customers will be: "Make your customers happy, increase your revenue."

It may be necessary to attend tech expositions, conferences, and trade shows to showcase the usefulness of Sanders Infotech services.

Financial Plan

Sanders Infotech will raise the initial capital for its business activities and hope to increase its revenue year-on-year for the first 3 years of operating. Customers will be able to pay monthly, quarterly, or annually for the services they enjoy from Sanders infotech.

The profits for the first 5 years will be reinvested in the business until Sanders files for an IPO.

Income Statement for a sample fiscal year ending December 31, 20XX

Revenue: $5 million

Total Expenses: $1 million

Net Income Before Taxes: $4 million

Statement of Financial Position as of December 31, 20XX

Cash and Cash Equivalents: $2 million

Receivables: $1 million

Property and Equipment: $2 million

Intangible Assets: $500,000

Total Assets: $5.5 million

Balance Statement

The board of directors is expected to approve the 20XX fiscal year budget for Sanders Infotech, which is estimated at $5 million in revenues and $1 million in expenditures. This reveals that the organization is profitable at the end of the fiscal year.

Cash Flow Statement for the Fiscal Year Ending December 31, 20XX

Operating Activities: Income Before Taxes -$500,000

Investing Activities: New equipment and supplies -$500,000

Raised capital = $5 million

Net Change in Cash: $4 million

According to the 20XX fiscal year financial statements for Sanders Infotech, the business' investments are projected to decrease by 5 percent, and it is projected to generate $5 million in revenues. Its total assets are valued at $5.5 million.

Appendix

This is where all other documents necessary for running Sunshine Forever will be placed.

Discussion Questions

1. Why it is essential to "know your numbers" while running a service business?

2. What should be included in an operational plan of a service business?

3. List two main ways a service business can market its services to prospective customers.

Quiz

1. **Which of these types of business plans require more investment in inventory and distribution?**
   a. Product business plan
   b. Service business plan
   c. I don't know

2. **Why is it important that a service business plan must contain a "detailed service description"?**
   a. So that customers can pay a higher price for services
   b. Investors and future partners can understand the exact services being offered
   c. It is a kind of advertisement

3. **What kind of CRM solution customers can enjoy by subscribing to Sanders Infotech's CRM 1?**
   a. Customer service telephony/communication
   b. Collection of customers' data and information
   c. An accounting for measuring revenue as a result of good customer service

4. If a company has a problem in effectively communicating with its customers, which of the Customer Relationship Management software should it purchase from Sanders Infotech?

a. CRM 2

b. CRM3

c. CRM 1

5. What is usually included in a service business's operation plan?

a. A cash flow statement

b. A detailed plan of day-to-day activities for running the service business operations

c. A mission statement

6. Technically, there is no difference between a marketing plan for a product business plan and a service business plan.

a. False

b. True

c. I don't know

7. The major strength of Sanders Infotech is that it has....

a. its own patented and proprietary CRM technologies

b. a good CEO

c. an investor

8. Which of the following factors does not contribute to the success of any tech business?

a. Its location

b. Having experienced tech professionals

c. Being able to provide services to customers globally

9. What segment of the market is Sanders Infotech serving?

a. Large companies

b. Huge multinationals

c. Small- to medium-sized businesses

10. Sanders Infotech spends $500,000 on intangible assets. Which of the following assets is considered an intangible asset?

a. Computers

b. Office building

c. Software

Answers	1 – a	2 – b	3 – b	4 – a	5 – b
	6 – b	7 – a	8 – a	9 – c	10 – c

Chapter Summary

- The fundamental difference between a product business plan and a service business plan is that for a service business, you spend little or no resources on inventory and distribution.
- To produce an effective service business plan, you should focus on four important things: Providing a detailed description of your service(s), having a full understanding of your finances, deploying a useful marketing strategy, and designing an efficient operational plan.
- A service business is customer-centric and should target the main customers that need its service(s).

References

- Genadinik, Alex (2015). Business plan template and example. How to write a business plan: Business planning made simple. Seattle: Amazon.

- Lah, Thomas, and Wood J.B. (2016). Technology-as-a-Service playbook: How to grow a profitable subscription business. Austin: Point B, Inc.

This page is intentionally left blank

Chapter 9

Business Plan for a Manufacturing Business

Manufacturing is an intensive business operation and therefore requires a special business plan. Due to the high degree of precision or standards demanded in manufacturing, every step of the manufacturing process must be highlighted and full of the necessary details. It would amount to a waste of financial and human resources if a manufacturing company operates without a definite plan. Such a company will manufacture products and/or services that will be subpar and rejected by many consumers. It becomes inevitable for manufacturers to have a guideline they can follow to the letter. In this section, you will identify the main elements of a manufacturing business plan and how to structure them to design a pragmatic business plan for a manufacturing business.

Key learning objectives should include the readers' understanding of the following:

- Understanding the Main Elements In A Business Plan for A Manufacturing Business
- A Sample Business Plan for A Manufacturing Business

9.1 Understanding the Main Elements in A Business Plan for A Manufacturing Business

A manufacturing business plan is different from the other types of business plans in many ways. Some of the main elements of a manufacturing business plan are described below:

1. **Facility and tangible assets:** You need to describe, in detail, the facilities and the tangible assets that your manufacturing business will be making use of. Some of these tangible assets may include but are not limited to equipment, factory buildings, vehicles, cash, and/or investments. It is impossible to run a successful manufacturing unit without a well-fitted factory or facility. Is the equipment up to the standards required in your chosen niche? Did you make sure that your facilities are designed according to the specifications expected by your industry? Investors need to find answers to these important questions in your business plan. So, if you fail to include all the essential information in your business, you may be seen as unprepared to run a manufacturing plant.

2. **Operational Plan:** Any other kind of business can be operated without any strict compliance with standards and ethics, but

manufacturing is different. Every business action that concerns a manufacturing plant must be guarded by well-defined procedures. More importantly, each operation must be carried out by qualified and experienced personnel or employees. In other businesses, anyone can run certain aspects of the business. However, in manufacturing, what an engineer needs to do cannot be assigned to a scientist, despite the fact that they are both well-educated. Precision is broadly expected in manufacturing, and this is why risks and mistakes are properly eliminated. How will you react to being sold a defective product? Won't you be very angry having paid a lot of money only to be sold a product that doesn't work well? This is why manufacturing demands carefulness at all stages of product production. Hence, your operational plan must be detail-oriented so that your prospective investors or partners can see all the necessary precautions you are going to take in order to produce only high-quality products.

3. **Marketing plan:** It is advisable that you include your sales plan in your manufacturing business's marketing plan. Getting your business's finished products into the hands of customers requires a smooth delivery or distribution system. Will you be selling your products directly to consumers or through retail/wholesale outlets? What means of advertising do you think will be effective for your prospective customers, traditional or digital marketing? The right approach is to choose to reach your customers through the most effective marketing method.

4. **Financial plan:** It costs a lot to start and manage a manufacturing business. You need to state clearly in your business plan how you hope to get the funds to start the business. More so, you should be able to give investors or partners a picture of what your business's financial prospects

look like. You will be expected to draw up a projected financial statement to support your claim that your manufacturing business will be profitable in the short- and long-term. It is also sensible to present a projected cash flow statement that removes any fear that your business may be cash-strapped. You can see why it is important that you know your numbers, and then present them to convey your message in your business plan. If you do not know how to prepare your projected financials, you may want to enlist the service of a business consultant or business development professional.

9.2 A Sample Business Plan for A Manufacturing Business

This sample business plan for a manufacturing business will provide you with the much-needed direction that you can follow while designing your own business plan. Use the information given in this sample as a guide but flesh it out with more information you have already gathered about your own manufacturing business.

Executive Summary

Lobat Manufacturing Company specializes in the production of toys and other playthings for babies under the age of 9. Owned by three partners, the company attempts to solve the problem of the scarcity of toys for children in the age range from 3 to 9 years old.

One of the main advantages of Lobat manufacturing over its competitors is that its distribution channels are efficient and fast;

the company can quickly get its toy products to consumers in a matter of weeks.

Company Overview

Registered as a limited partnership, Lobat Manufacturing's ownership is owned equally among the three owners.

The company's manufacturing plant is located in London, United Kingdom.

Lobat Manufacturing is established to bring smiles to the faces of the little children who may find it difficult to obtain useful toys they could play with.

Since the demographics served by the company is huge, Lobat Manufacturing is expected to break even (in profits) within 3-5 years of operation.

Business Description

Parents of children aged 3-9 often struggle to get nice toys for their kids. They are mostly advised to use those for older children. As a result of this, kids between the ages of 3 and 9 don't necessarily feel comfortable playing with toys meant for their older brothers and sisters. Lobat Manufacturing takes it upon itself to research, design, and manufacture toys that perfectly suit this demographic.

The toys, mostly stuffed animals and plastic playthings are designed to be naturally attractive to kids who are 3-9 years old.

They are priced affordably, and this is one of the sales propositions, because other toys in the market are either too expensive or not available.

Lobat Manufacturing will work with some suppliers that would provide the much-needed raw materials and distributors (wholesalers) who will help sell the toys.

Market Analysis

The toy market for children aged 3-9 is not as crowded as those for younger and older kids. This market segment has a good prospect of expanding within the next 5 years.

Even though other toy manufacturers still remain formidable competitors, all the toys made by Lobat Manufacturing have in-built proprietary chips that make it possible for the toys to move, speak, walk, and dance. These features will attract the little kids and make Lobat Manufacturing's toys "hot cakes" in the marketplace.

The major weakness confronted by the company is in raising enough capital to buy automated machines or equipment that could mass-produce these toys. Therefore, the company will be starting its operations using some simple, hand-operated machines, which can only produce a few toys per day.

Operating Plan

The day-to-day operations at Lobat Manufacturing will be managed by experienced and hardworking professionals who have had at least 3 years of experience in toy manufacturing.

The company will set up a manufacturing plant in London and work with suppliers and distributors globally. The company has already signed contracts with some suppliers and wholesalers and will work towards increasing the number of its sales channels in the next 1-2 years.

Lobat Manufacturing will not be selling directly to parents; however, it will use distributors and wholesalers, including major retail stores around the globe.

Marketing and Sales Plan

Since Lobat Manufacturing is only selling to major distributors and wholesalers, much of the company's marketing activities will be directed toward them. This may involve using both traditional and digital marketing and participating in expositions, conferences, and trade shows to showcase toys to prospective distributors.

Financial Plan

You should understand that this financial plan is a sample for you so that you can understand how to format yours properly. Therefore, you will need to obtain some numbers about your company to use in calculating your income statement, statement of financial position, balance statement, and cash flow statement.

Income Statement for a sample fiscal year ending December 31, 20XX

Revenue: $10 million

Total Expenses: $6 million

Net Income Before Taxes: $4 million

Statement of Financial Position as of December 31, 20XX

Cash and Cash Equivalents: $3 million

Receivables: $1 million

Property and Equipment: $1 million

Intangible Assets: $500,000

Total Assets: $5.5 million

Balance Statement

The board of directors is expected to approve the 20XX fiscal year budget for Lobat Manufacturing which is estimated at $10 million in revenues and $6 million in expenditures. This reveals that the organization is profitable at the end of the fiscal year.

Cash Flow Statement for the Fiscal Year Ending December 31, 20XX

Operating Activities: Income Before Taxes -$1 million

Investing Activities: New equipment and supplies -$1 million

Raised capital = $12 million

Net Change in Cash: $10 million

According to the 20XX fiscal year financial statements for Lobat Manufacturing, the business's investments is projected to increase by 2%, and it is projected to generate $10 million in revenues. Its total assets are valued at $5.5 million.

Appendix

This is where all other documents necessary for running Lobat Manufacturing will be placed.

Discussion Questions

1. Why should a manufacturing business have a well-defined operational plan?
2. Does Lobat Manufacturing have a great financial statement?
3. What is the main strength of Lobat Manufacturing when compared with its rivals?

Quiz

1. **What market demographic is Lobat Manufacturing producing toys for?**
   a. 1-2 year-olds
   b. 10-12 year-olds
   c. 3-9 year-olds

2. **Which of the following tangible assets is quite useful in manufacturing?**
   a. Office building
   b. Equipment
   c. Table

3. **How does Lobat Manufacturing plan to sell its products?**
   a. Via a distributor
   b. Direct-to-consumer
   c. Through mailing

4. **The major weakness of the company when compared with its competitors is a/an:**
   a. Inability to raise enough capital for automated machinery
   b. Lack of qualified engineers
   c. Incomplete facility

5. What type of toys will the company be manufacturing?

a. Wooden toys

b. Stuffed toys and plastic playthings

c. Paper crafts

6. What is the legal structure of Lobat Manufacturing?

a. It is a limited partnership

b. It is a limited liability company

c. It is a sole proprietorship

7. Lobat Manufacturing is located in....

a. New Zealand

b. London

c. South Korea

8. Looking at the company's finances, how much does Lobat Manufacturing raise from investors?

a. $10 million

b. $5million

c. $12million

9. Lobat Manufacturing is owned by .... businesspeople.

a. 4

b. 9

c. 3

10. According to its financials, Lobat Manufacturing's total assets amount to....

a. $10 million

b. $5.5 million

c. $8million

Answers	1 – a	2 – b	3 – a	4 – a	5 – b
	6 – a	7 – b	8 – c	9 – c	10 – b

Chapter Summary

- When writing a business plan for a manufacturing company, it is very important to highlight the company's facilities, tangible assets such as equipment, organizational processes, and its financials.
- Manufacturing businesses must have a definite market segment they aim to serve before going into production. It is not sensible to manufacture a product first before looking for where to sell it or who will be interested in it.
- It is also important to highlight the marketing and sales plan within the business plan.

References

- Liraz, Meir. (2020). Starting a manufacturing business: Complete business plan template. Seattle: Amazon.

- Selikoff, Steven. (2020). The complete book of product design, development, manufacturing, and sales. Washington State: Product Development Academy.

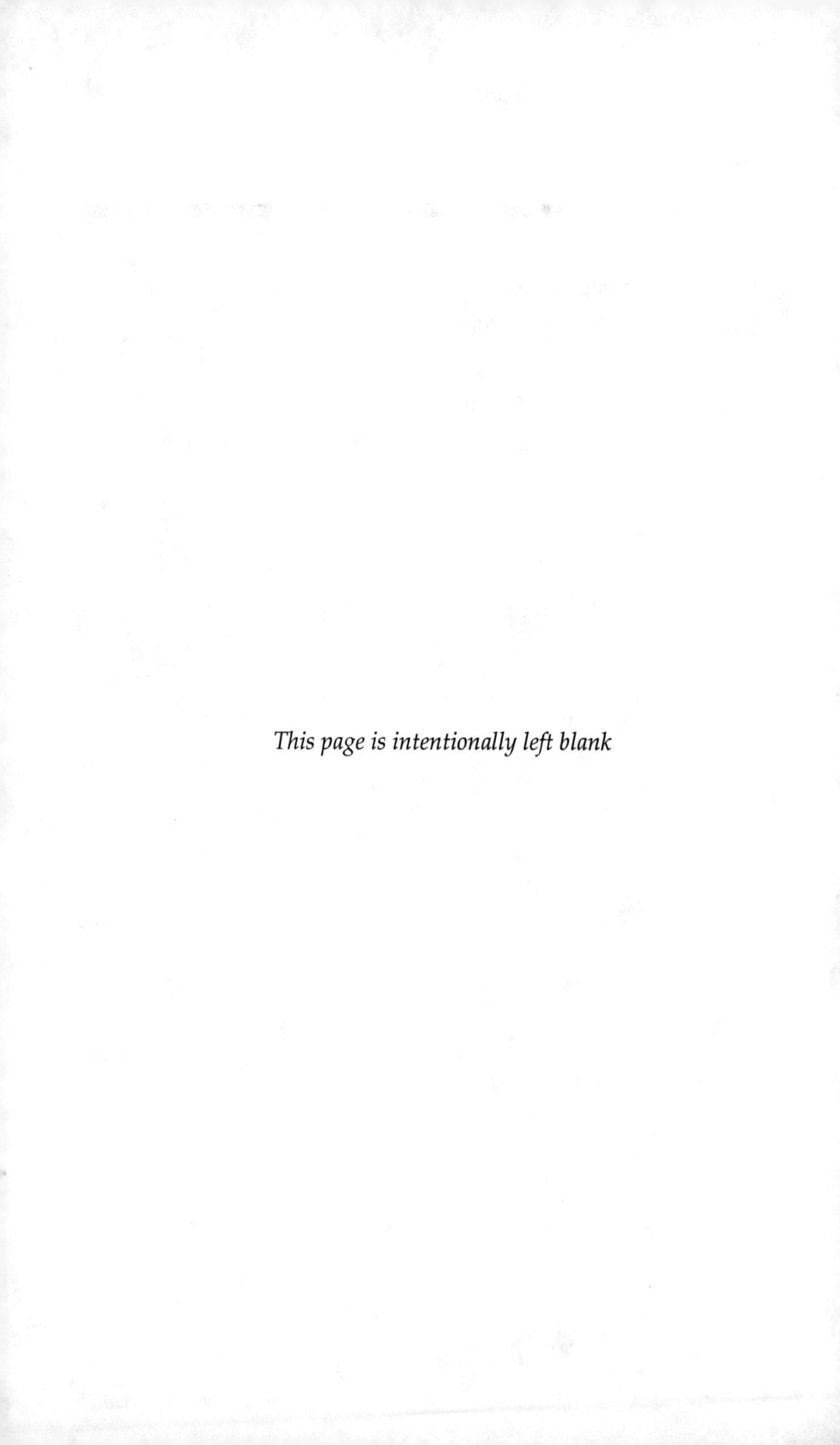

This page is intentionally left blank

Chapter **10**

Business Plan for Project Development

Project management is a specialized field or endeavor on its own and, as such, you need to prepare a specific business plan for it. It doesn't matter whether you are writing a business plan for construction, computer, or even manufacturing projects: they all have something in common, which is discussed below in detail.

Key learning objectives should include the readers' understanding of the following:

- How to Write An Effective Business Plan for Project Management
- A Sample Business Plan for Project Management

10.1 How to Write An Effective Business Plan for Project Management

To start with, the words "project management" can be simply defined as the process of managing a project, irrespective of its nature or type. Hence, if you want to successfully manage a project, these four important aspects need to be considered.

- **Operational Plan:** The most significant aspect of your project management business plan is its operational plan. This is the blueprint or summary of the actions that would be taken in completing the project. You will be required to describe the approaches you will be taking to see that the project is satisfactorily completed. More so, you will also need to showcase the experiences and skills of the professionals or employees who will be working on the project. Are you going to execute the project in a specific location, facility, or a manufacturing plant? Then, you must state that in the business plan. It is reasonable to say that the strength of your operational plan reveals how ready you are to successfully carry out the project. In fact, many investors or prospective partners would like to know how the project will proceed from start to finish—you only have one chance to let them know about it, and that should be incorporated into your organizational plan.

- **Financials:** In practice, many projects are left uncompleted. You can see many of those uncompleted projects around you. Why did the people working on them fail to complete them? The answer to this very important question is not far-fetched. When those who were involved in drafting the plan to do the project were on the drawing board, they might have undervalued how much it would cost them to successfully execute the project. So, in the middle of the project, they might discover they did not have enough funds to see the project to completion, and chose to abandon it. It is true that most business plans are prepared based on projections; however, the case is different for project management. You must come up with the exact cost of doing the project. You can adopt the following five procedures to precisely estimate the cost of your project:

- First, you should compile all the necessary tasks and the resources that you will be using to complete the project.
- Based on your team's capability, allocate resources to all the required tasks.
- You should also need to estimate how long the project will take to be completed. So, designing a project schedule is mandatory.
- You should select a specific cost estimation method to calculate the exact cost of the project. You may even want to check out a related project and discover how much it cost to produce such a similar project.
- Use a budget tracker once you have started working on the project to make sure you are operating within budget and monitoring the progress of the project.

- **Market Analysis:** If you are undertaking the project for yourself or your own business, it is advisable to pay attention to the results of your market analysis. In this case, you would like to fully understand your strengths, weaknesses, opportunities, and threats (SWOT). If you feel that you are in a better place to outperform your competitors, it may be a great opportunity for you to pursue the business idea. However, where there are more threats against the project you are planning to execute, it is reasonable to avoid taking on such a project. You may end up losing more money than you are earning from such a venture. Over the years, project managers or project management consultants have found creative ways to identify which projects are profitable and worth their time. If a project will cause your business to lose a lot of its resources, both monetary and human capital, it is not sensible to pursue it.

- **Business Description:** It is imperative that you should describe exactly what your business aims to achieve and how you are going to accomplish it. How much will you be pricing your services? And how are your customers going to feel satisfied with the quality of the job your company has done for them? Are the opportunities in your niche huge or not? Take your time to offer clear and understandable descriptions of your services in your business plan.

10.2 A Sample Business Plan for Project Management

Any business plan for project management that doesn't address, in detail, the main three elements described above may be considered ineffective. You don't want to appear to an investor as someone who doesn't have a deep understanding of what he/she aims to accomplish.

There is a sample given below that you could imitate, though you will still be required to do your homework, gather enough data about your available resources and tasks, and sit down to prepare your business plan.

Executive Summary

Star Consultants is a project management company established to operate in the educational industry. Its primary duties are to help schools and academic institutions to design and build school buildings.

Star Consultants believes in quality and usefulness, making sure that all the school building projects they work on are great and long-lasting.

Company Overview

Star Consultants is a Limited Liability Company owned by five members (entrepreneurs) in Ontario, Canada. The company hopes to become a force in the educational industry by helping schools design and erect strong buildings that will last forever.

The Company has been in operation for a couple of years but hopes to expand its services to several cities in Canada. It is adopting the latest technologies in building construction and hiring highly qualified engineers and professionals to be able to meet its set goals in the next five years.

Business Description

Star Consultants help schools, ranging from kindergartens to universities to design and build school buildings that include classrooms, laboratories, libraries, halls, and so on. In fact, the

Company works with its customers to design and budget the projects, and eventually complete the erection of the school buildings.

Market Analysis

Focusing only on academic buildings gives Star Consultants a greater opportunity to develop its influence on customers that need the kinds of services it offers. More so, the Company can concentrate its resources on that niche/industry, performing better year on year.

The major weakness of the Company is that the niche is narrow—people don't get to build new school buildings every year. So, Star Consultants has discovered a new way to monetize its services by offering building renovations and beautifications to its customers. Incidentally, this new kind of service has helped the Company increase its profits three-fold and remain sustainable.

Operation Plan

In order to successfully execute its customers' projects, Star Consultants follow these important steps:

- Initial meeting to discuss the scope of the project
- Draft the preliminary costs of the project
- Have the second meeting with the customer to talk about project requirements and cost
- Getting the resources ready
- Starting building

- Managing the budget
- Completing the project

Star Consultants ensures that the school buildings it works on conform strictly with standards in the industry.

The Company uses the latest building technologies to carry out its works. This, in turn, leads to high-quality performance on the part of the Company.

Marketing and Sales Plan

Star Consultants engage both in digital and traditional advertising to promote its services. More importantly, happy customers who truly appreciate what the Company has done for them automatically become its arduous marketers through word of mouth.

Star Consultants also participate in expositions, conferences, and trade shows to meet prospective customers.

Financial Plan

After gathering all the necessary financial data about the business's activities, you will need to present them in tables that can be understandable to anyone who glances through your business plan. You should understand that this financial plan is a sample for you so that you can understand how to design yours.

Make sure you showcase your business's income statement, statement of financial position, balance statement, and cash flow statement.

Income Statement for a sample fiscal year ending December 31, 20XX

Revenue: $2 million

Total Expenses: $1 million

Net Income Before Taxes: $1 million

Statement of Financial Position as of December 31, 20XX

Cash and Cash Equivalents: $1 million

Receivables: $500,000

Property and Equipment: $500,000

Intangible Assets: $100,000

Total Assets: $2.1 million

Balance Statement

The board of directors is expected to approve the 20XX fiscal year budget for Star Consultants which is estimated at $2 million in revenues and $1 million in expenditures. This shows that the organization is profitable at the end of the fiscal year.

Cash Flow Statement for the Fiscal Year Ending December 31, 20XX

Operating Activities: Income Before Taxes -$1 million

Investing Activities: New equipment and supplies -$500,000

Raised capital = $3 million

Net Change in Cash: $1.5 million

According to the 20XX fiscal year financial statements for Star Consultants, the business' investments is projected to increase by 1 percent, and it is projected to generate $2 million in revenues. Its total assets are valued at $2.1 million.

Appendix

This is where all other documents necessary for running Star Consultants will be placed.

Discussion Questions

1. Why is it necessary to have a well-defined operational plan in a project management business plan?

2. What kinds of data must you have before you can properly prepare your project management business's financials?

3. What is the best way for a project management business to advertise its services?

Quiz

1. **Which of these services is offered by Star Consultants?**
   a. Travel
   b. Road construction
   c. School buildings

2. **What should be included in an operational plan for a project management business plan?**
   a. Mission statement
   b. The exact procedures for carrying out the project
   c. Names of investors

3. **Which of these kinds of buildings is not undertaken by Star Consultants?**
   a. Church building
   b. Classroom
   c. School laboratory

4. **Star Consultants plans to expand its operations to several cities in Canada.**
   a. True
   b. False
   c. I don't know

5. **One of the commonest reasons a project may be left uncompleted is that....**

    a. The project managing company runs out of resources

    b. The company does not stick to its mission statement

    c. The customer wants to change the initial plan

6. **How much capital did Star Consultants raise for its business operations?**

    a. $3million

    b. $1million

    c. $500,000

7. **What additional service does the Company offer its customers?**

    a. School renovations

    b. Road construction

    c. Glassmaking

8. **How would you describe the niche that Star Consultants serve?**

    a. I think it is a narrow niche

    b. I think it is broad niche

    c. I don't know

9. According to the Company's financials, how much revenue did it make?

a. $5million

b. $2million

c. $500,000

10. The Company does the following to ensure quality in its business operations, except:

a. By using the latest technologies

b. By complying with the standards in the industry

c. By taking on more investors

Answers	1 – c	2 – b	3 – a	4 – a	5 – c
	6 – a	7 – a	8 – a	9 – b	10 – c

Chapter Summary

- The four main elements of a project management business plan are its operational plan, service description, financials, and market analysis.
- It is imperative that efforts must be deployed to developing the operational plan to avoid experiencing any problems while developing the projects.
- The services offered by the Company are meant to promote the business activities of its clients.

References

- Graham, Nick. (2014). *Project management checklists for dummies.* New Jersey: For Dummies Publisher.

- Rose, Molly Elodie. (2020). *Business plan for project management consulting.* Seattle: Amazon.

This page is intentionally left blank

Conclusion

This book offers a glimpse into how a good business plan can be developed. As a useful guide, it will take you step by step through the necessary steps required to write a business plan that is effective and up-to-date.

Every step is simplified enough to be replicated by anyone, irrespective of their levels of experiences in business writing. The best way to gain much insight from the book is to follow it one step at a time.

Do not rush through it because you may miss some important pieces of advice provided in it. If at any time you are confused about what to do next when producing your business plan, always come back to the book for proper instructions.

This page is intentionally left blank

Appendix

Who Are Business Consultants and What Do They Do?

Business consultants or business development experts are professionals whose primary duty is to help you develop your business idea and provide a clear roadmap about how to smoothly turn your ideas/concepts into a flourishing business.

Since the 1990s, the functions carried out by business consultants for their clients have significantly increased, and they include:

- **Business planning:** You will need to sit down with your business consultant or business development manager to plan your business. You will receive all the necessary assistance about how to design and document your business plan. At this stage, you will be required to explain everything you want to achieve with your business to your business consultant who, in turn, will guide you with the right steps to take in actualizing your entrepreneurial dreams or aspirations. Having a brilliant idea is not enough to start a thriving business. It requires establishing structures and following due processes. If you are an undergraduate or graduate student who has been inspired to change the world, you should not commit the same mistakes that some other would-entrepreneurs had made in the past. You should spend some time with a business development consultant and create a realistic business plan. You will surely discover that some things that you didn't previously know about will start manifesting or revealing themselves to you. That's the power of brainstorming. You can't do that alone!

- **Business advisory:** Nowadays, it is not new to see business consultants advising their clients on various aspects of managing or running a business. These may include but are not limited to offering creative pieces of advice on how to legally set up a business, recruiting, budgeting, production, payroll, and promotional campaigns. Those steps are what will make or break your business. In the United States, you are required to legally register your business. If you, out of ignorance, set up the wrong legal entity, you are likely going to spend more money running the enterprise. In the same way, a business development consultant can offer constructive pieces of advice on how to recruit the best and most skillful employees for your business. A lot of companies are stagnant and inability to innovate due to the fact that they have uninspiring employees. The parlance in the business circle is that if you hired wrong, your business is already leaping on the wrong foot! One main issue you should avoid at all costs is defaulting in paying taxes or not having adequate knowledge about which taxes to pay. Working with a business development consultant can help you eliminate all those confusions.
- **Business improvement:** A good business consultant will continuously gather information that will improve his/her client's businesses. For example, your business consultant

may advise you about some new and transformative operational methods, refined technologies, and concepts that will immensely improve your business operations. Every huge company today was once a startup. In other words, before they reach their current growth state, it indicates that they have taken serious measures to refine their technologies and operational procedures. It is true that a new entrepreneur or business owner doesn't have all the answers when starting out. However, you cannot remain in the startup phase forever—you will need to grow exponentially to achieve your business objectives. When you choose to work with an experienced and knowledgeable business development consultant, he/she will help you iron out the required steps you need to take to boost growth in your venture.

- **Business performance:** Your business consultant may also develop some key performance indicators (KPIs) for your business and periodically measure them to see that your business is doing well in relation to all the metrics. Normally, not all companies have internal metrics to measure their operational performances. This is why you don't have to wait too long to onboard a business consultant who will work with you every step of the way to analyze your business processes and come up with standardized metrics to measure performance. If you don't monitor your performance, how in the world will you know if your business is growing or not?

- **Business continuity:** If you work with a business consultant for a long time, such a consultant may also come to your rescue when your business is facing some serious problems or confronting uncertainties that may threaten your business's survival. There is a reason why even businesses with household names still work with business development consultants—continuity! There is a saying that you cannot afford to sit on a path (even if you have found the right one!) because other people using the same path will stampede and crush you! It doesn't matter how great and prosperous your company is, you cannot be resting your oars on that—keep growing and keep innovating. If you are complacent and unwilling to innovate, other smaller companies or newly established startups will overtake you and snap your market share out of your hands.

As described above, a good and supportive business consultant can go a long way to helping your business grow quickly and profitably. It all depends on your working relationship with the consultant.

While selecting a business consultant, it is advisable that you pay serious attention to his/her past experiences in the industry related to yours, and his/her track records in the businesses that the consultant has previously worked with.

Online Business Resources

No one runs a business alone; you will need to rely on some assistance from people who have successfully run their own businesses before you. The internet is a big school for entrepreneurs to learn from. Whatever your learning objectives, you can find useful resources online that will guide you in making good decisions about your businesses. Highlighted below are some online business resources you could take advantage of:

- **Blogs:** You can learn a lot by reading blogs written by entrepreneurs, business publications, and academic articles. Here are four nuggets of wisdom you can obtain by reading business blogs:
    - **Practical advice:** Most business blogs or blogs about some areas of business operation offer unique practical guidance you can learn a lot from. For instance, if you are having a hard time doing your bookkeeping, you can search online for blogs that deal with that subject matter. You should only spend time reading blogs by business people who are possibly going through the same experience as yours or have dealt with such an issue before while running their businesses.
    - **Different perspectives:** For every matter, there are different perspectives. When you read business publications, you are picking up new, diverse ideas from the writers. Doing this regularly will widen your horizon and turn you into a professional. For example, there are different approaches to running a startup or company; you can learn exactly how others are doing it and what outcomes they are getting. If you fancy any of those outcomes, you may want to do the same in your business to achieve the same results.
    - **Confidence boosting:** By acquiring more knowledge about your industry or market and taking defined steps highlighted in the blogs you are reading, you will in no time become confident in whatever you are doing. We are living in the digital age where almost all answers to our problems can be found free of charge online. Just Google it or YouTube it! What is interesting about this approach is that you don't have to attend physical

seminars, workshops, or conferences to update your knowledge in any aspect of entrepreneurship.

  - **Permanent reference:** Blogs are kinds of permanent references; it means you bookmark and always return to them whenever you want to refresh your understanding. This entails that, unlike seminars or workshops, you won't be asked to pay to attend each time you consult those blogs you had found to be quite useful.

- **YouTube:** You can watch YouTube videos to teach yourself how to work on certain aspects of your business operations. Among all video-hosting and streaming platforms, YouTube stands out in the sense that it offers a wide variety of self-learning alternatives. If you want to gain more from YouTube videos, follow these essential steps:

  - **Subscription:** YouTube subscription is still pretty much free. All you need to do is to click on that red "subscribe" icon and move up to request a notification for all the videos the channels you will be uploading in the future. This singular action will save you from missing some important videos in the future.

  - **Niche videos:** It will amount to a waste of time to spend hours sitting in front of your computer watching all YouTube videos. You can search for niche videos and subscribe to those channels or one or two leading channels in your desired niche. You will be able to spend quality time on YouTube if you watch only selected videos that address the pain points you are researching solutions for.

  - **Time management:** Even after choosing the most related and instructional videos to watch, you still have to work on time management. Watching YouTube can be addictive; if you don't have a lot of time to stare at your computer consuming videos, you may want to plan how many hours you could afford to watch YouTube videos per week.

- **Free eBooks:** Now you can have access to free business eBooks on several platforms online. Some of the places you can free business eBooks online include but are not limited to:
- **Amazon Kindle Store:** Amazon offers both paid and free eBooks on different subject matters. You can search the Amazon Kindle marketplace for eBooks on any topics that you want. The Free Popular Classics page has a list of Top 100 Best Sellers in all genres.
- **Apple Book Store:** You can also find a free selection of eBook titles on the Apple Book Store. You can access free titles by going to the Free Books tab in the sidebar. The free eBooks are divided into different categories.
- **Google Play Bookstore:** You can easily free books on Google Play by just entering "free eBooks" in the search bar.
- **Barnes & Noble Online:** Barnes & Noble online is the digital platform whereby Barnes & Noble produces its eBooks and display them for sale. On this same platform, precisely on their NOOK Reading App, you can search for some free eBooks based on your desired topics.
- **Kobo Bookstore:** Owned by Rakuten, Kobo literary e-tailer also hosts some free eBooks that anyone can access free of charge. You will need to download the Kobo App.

- **Free-Ebooks.net:** This platform has thousands of free eBooks anyone can access at no cost. You can check out Free-eBooks' Classics Package.
- **Project Gutenberg:** This is a huge digital archive of books and eBooks that was reportedly founded in 1971. It currently has over 60,000 documents and books that can all be accessed for free.
- **Open Culture:** You can find free eBooks on this platform, most especially those little classics of famous authors.
- **Freebooksy:** This is a very popular book promotion site. It is a hub site that links out to many free eBooks sites. The good thing about Freebooksy is that it only focuses on "free eBooks".
- **BookBub:** Under the "Readers" tab, you can click "Free Ebooks". BookBub is also a promotional site, which means that it generally links to other sites that host free books for readers.
- **ManyBooks:** These eBooks on this site are 100% free, and they come in various genres.To save time, you may want to check out the "Editor's Choice" for high-quality books that are worth reading.

NOTE: Even though many news outlets or business newspaper and magazine publishers are asking people to pay for their content, you can still access most of the back numbers (previous publications) for free. If you are looking for some scholarly publications on business activities, Google Scholar offers many options for readers.

Books and Articles

Here are some books and articles where you could discover some vital information that is related to the business plan you are writing. The books and articles touch on some key elements of a business plan, based on your chosen niches/industry as well as some general ideas you can incorporate into your business plan in order to make it very effective.

Graham, Nick. (2014). *Project management checklists for dummies.* New Jersey: For Dummies Publisher.

Rose, Molly Elodie. (2020). *Business plan for project management consulting.* Seattle: Amazon.

Liraz, Meir. (2020). *Starting a manufacturing business: Complete business plan template.* Seattle: Amazon.

Selikoff, Steven. (2020). *The complete book of product design, development, manufacturing, and sales.* Washington State: Product Development Academy.

Genadinik, Alex (2015). *Business plan template and example. How to write a business plan: Business planning made simple.* Seattle: Amazon.

Lah, Thomas, and Wood J.B. (2016). *Technology-as-a-Service playbook: How to grow a profitable subscription business.* Austin: Point B, Inc.

Anheier, Helmut, K. (2014). *Nonprofit organizations: Theory, management, policy.* New York: Routledge.

Heyman, Darian, R. (2016). *Nonprofit fundraising 101: A practical guide to easy-to-implement ideas and tips from industry experts.* New Jersey: Wiles & Sons.

Genadinik, Alex. (2015). *How to write a business plan: Business planning made simple.* Seattle: Amazon.

Horan, Jim. (2019). *The one page business plan professional consultant edition.* Seattle: Amazon.

Porter, Michael E. (1998). *Competitive strategies: Techniques for analyzing industries and competitors.* Washington, DC: Free Press.

Stevens, Robert E., Loudon David L, Sherwood Philip K, and Dunn John Paul (2006). *Market opportunity analysis: Text and Cases.* New York: Routledge.

Gallegos, J. (2019). Business plan 101. A guide to combine technical, financial, operational and marketing data that will not only get you funded but will actually help you operate your business successfully. Seattle: Amazon.

Levinson, Conrad J, and Levinson, J. (2008). Startup guide to guerrilla marketing: A simple battle plan for first-time marketers. California: Entrepreneur Press.

Brennan, K. (2019). Startup CFO: The finance handbook for your growing business. Seattle: Amazon.

Murphy, Chris B. (2022). "Understanding the Cash Flow Statement." *Investopedia. https://www.investopedia.com/investing/what-is-a-cash-flow-statement/*

Bryant, S. (2020). "How many startups fail and why?" *Investopedia. https://www.investopedia.com/articles/personal-finance/040915/how-many-startups-fail-and-why.asp#:~:text=Research%20concludes%20*

21.5%25%20of%20startups%20fail%20in%20the,and%20not%20 being%20an%20expert%20in%20the%20industry.

White, Richard M. (2014). *The Entrepreneur's Manual: Business Start-Ups, Spin-Offs, and Innovative Management.* Kent: Churchill and Dunn Ltd.

Small Business Help: Where to Find Helpful Advice for Your Business

In addition to the resources outlined above, there are still some avenues where you could find helpful advice concerning how to successfully run a business. These include:

- **Local business agency or office:** Some cities or towns have a local business agency that offers free business to business owners living in that jurisdiction. Their services range from providing free office space to teaching entrepreneurs tricks for managing a profitable business. Every year, some cities budget a certain amount of money to support local businesses. This money is made available to the local business agency or office to provide maximum support for any startups or struggling businesses in that jurisdiction. So, don't feel reluctant to contact them for help. In fact, they are always looking out to assist new entrepreneurs.
- **Incubators:** Business incubators help entrepreneurs develop or fine-tune their business ideas during what looks like a short-term apprenticeship. Business owners will learn different approaches to running a great company while their incubating period lasts. When signing up with an incubator, make sure you fully understand the contractual agreements.

While some incubators offer their services for free, others may request an equity in your business. You don't want to be confused about this term of agreement later.

- **Independent product development agency:** Entrepreneurs can get some assistance from some independent agencies that offer product development opportunities. Most of these agencies charge for their services, but in most cases, they may reduce their service charges or pick up some equity in the business instead of receiving monetary compensation.

www.ingramcontent.com/pod-product-compliance
Lightning Source LLC
Chambersburg PA
CBHW070324270326
41926CB00017B/3757
* 9 7 8 1 6 3 6 5 1 1 2 1 4 *